COBBLESTONE'S

New York
City Reader

A Collection From the Pages

of *Cobblestone* and *Faces* Magazines

Cobblestone Publishing Company

Peterborough, New Hampshire

Cover: Colored engraving of Broadway in 1855, looking south from City Hall Park. The Granger Collection.
Back cover: Fireworks over Brooklyn Bridge in celebration of its 100th anniversary, 1983. © Curtis Willocks.

Editorial Development: Summer Street Press
Design: CPorter Designs
Photo Research: Linda Rill
Proofreading: Barbara Jatkola

Acknowledgments
The publisher gratefully acknowledges permission to reprint the following copyrighted material:

"Stars": Copyright © 1947 by Langston Hughes. Reprinted from *Don't You Turn Back* by permission of Alfred A. Knopf, New York.

"Sesame Noodles": Recipe adapted from *From the Earth: Chinese Vegetarian Cooking* by Eileen Yin-Fei Lo. Copyright © 1995 by Macmillan Publishing, New York.

Cobblestone Publishing Company
Simon & Schuster Education Group
7 School Street
Peterborough, NH 03458

Manufactured in the United States of America
ISBN 0-382409-61-2

1 2 3 4 5 6 7 8 9
97 98 99 00 01

Contents

From the Editors

[handwritten: 1997 published]

Do you know how New York City's famous nickname "the Big Apple" evolved? The term was used by a sports reporter in the 1920s in his articles about the Big Apple New York City racetracks, as well as by jazz performers in the 1920s and 1930s. In both cases, the phrase meant making or hitting "the big time." Over the years, the nickname has become synonymous with this exciting city.

[handwritten: not so 2010]

New York is both an old and a new city. The quiet chapel where George Washington worshiped in the 1700s stands near the soaring modern towers of Wall Street. Once open farmland inhabited by American Indians, the city is now famous for its modern skyscrapers and grid-patterned streets. It is home to more than seven million people and has become an international center for business and finance. The five boroughs making up the city, which were once separate islands, are now connected through a series of tunnels, bridges, ferries, and an underground subway system.

New York's neighborhoods are one of its strongest features. Since the 1600s, immigrants have introduced their customs, traditions, and foods, giving the city a lively international flavor. Neighborhoods and restaurants throughout the city reflect these different cultures, which range from Indian and Chinese to Italian and Spanish to Middle Eastern and Ethiopian.

New York attracts millions of visitors each year. Besides its world-famous restaurants, the city offers museums, Broadway shows, famous sites and historic buildings, and national and international sporting events. All aspects of the city are not glamorous, however. It is also home to a number of homeless and unemployed people, creating a sharp contrast to the wealthy and comfortable lifestyle enjoyed by some New Yorkers.

In this book, we introduce you to some of the people, places, and events associated with the Big Apple. New York City is your home. As you travel around your neighborhood and other parts of the city, decide for yourself whether the nickname fits.

The majority of the articles that appear in this reader were selected from issues of *Cobblestone: American History for Kids* and *Faces: People, Places, and Cultures.*

Early New York City

WHEN DID THIS GREAT CITY — ONE OF THE WORLD'S MOST IMPORTANT cities — actually begin? That's a question with more than one answer.

Some might say that New York City got its start when it received its name. That was in 1664, when English warships entered the harbor. They claimed the city for England and named it New York City, for the duke of York. ✳ 1604

Others might mention the year 1624. That was when a group of Dutch traders bought Manhattan Island from a group of Algonquian Indians. Of course, many Indians had lived on that island for hundreds, probably thousands, of years. Humans have made Manhattan their home for longer than written records have been kept.

Come on a tour of old New York City. Join Peter Stuyvesant as he walks along the dirt streets of Dutch New Amsterdam. Meet the Loyalists — colonists who supported the British during the American Revolution — as they help

British troops capture the city in 1776.

You can meet George Washington in early New York City, too. When he became the first president of the United States, New York was the young country's capital city. And New York is where Martha Washington became the first First Lady.

One street has meant more to the country's business than any other. Take a walk down historic Wall Street. There, for more than two hundred years, American companies have gotten the money they need to invest in new opportunities.

Not far from Wall Street lies a fascinating site. On Broadway, between Duane and Reade streets, archaeologists in 1991 found the remains of an African American cemetery. As many as twenty thousand people may have been buried there between 1712 and 1792.

In the late 1700s, New York City was just one of several major American towns. By the middle of the 1800s, it was by far the largest city in the country. What helped bring that change about was a narrow ditch, filled with water, that stretched from Lake Erie to the Hudson River. Take a trip down the Erie Canal and listen to a song that was sung by the people who worked its barges.

As you finish your tour of early New York, you will have a chance to create a time line. You will see just how closely the history of this great city is tied to the history of the United States.

2

The City's Dutch Roots

BY SANDRA DEDEN

[handwritten annotations: 1647, Peter Stuyvesant, from Holland]

Beneath the mirrored skyscrapers and the paved grid of Manhattan's streets today lies the story of another Manhattan. In 1624, the island was home to the Dutch, who called it New Amsterdam and the surrounding area New Netherland. These first settlers did not come to the New World to gain freedom to practice their religion as the Puritans did. Instead, they arrived as representatives of the Dutch West India Company, intent on making money in the fur trade.

Peter Stuyvesant arrived in Manhattan in 1647. He was the new director general of New Amsterdam and had sailed across the Atlantic Ocean from Holland. The island he saw was very different from the one we know today. It was a wild island, covered with lush green trees, broad fertile meadows, wild turkeys, partridge, and other animals.

Many different Algonquian tribes lived and hunted on the island. After they sold it to the Dutch, some Algonquians continued to live on the island with the colonists. There were frequent disputes between the colonists and the Indians, which occasionally erupted into wars.

Stuyvesant arrived as peace treaties were being negotiated and spent the next seventeen years trying to establish order. In 1664, he surrendered New Amsterdam to an invading English fleet.

If you use your imagination, you can still walk along the streets of Stuyvesant's New Amsterdam. The walk begins at East Tenth Street, between Third and Second avenues, on the outskirts of Greenwich Village. The neighborhood streets are quiet and lined with trees and three-story

This portrait of Peter Stuyvesant, which includes his signature, shows the leader of New Amsterdam in the 1660s.

brick apartment buildings. A small sign near 126 East Tenth Street marks the spot where Stuyvesant lived on his *bouwery* (farm). In 1854, historians found the stone rubble of the foundation of his house here.

When Stuyvesant wanted to go into town, he walked along a dirt road we now call the Bowery, named for his farm. The Bowery led him to the heart of New Amsterdam. Today it leads to the heart of Wall Street, the financial center of New York City. On his way, he passed what is now the corner of Water and Dover streets, close to where the Brooklyn Bridge stands today. Instead of the bridge, he saw and greeted a man named Cornelis Dircksen. Dircksen rowed passengers back and forth from Manhattan to Brooklyn for seven cents each way. If Stuyvesant followed Water Street, he would come to the end of the island, Pearl Street, which the colonists named for all the seashells found here.

Passing by the trading ships in the harbor, Stuyvesant might have headed toward downtown New Amsterdam, located along Beaver, Bridge (Brug), and Stone streets. These streets still have their original names today. Along these streets of dirt and mud stood the small one-story wooden buildings of the fifteen homes, two taverns, firehouse, and brewery of the West India Company. Many of the homes had small vegetable patches and fruit trees. The colonists' animals — pigs, cows, goats, and dogs —

hard to imagine

often wandered through the streets. The sounds of Dutch punctuated with French, Italian, American Indian, and African dialects filled the air.

easy

Stuyvesant might then have headed back inland toward the wall. We know it as Wall Street. The wall ran east to west across the island, "walling" out the wilderness and potential invaders to the north. Many colonists considered the wall a joke and sometimes ran their livestock through it to prove their point. The colonists and the West India Company argued over who was responsible for the wall's upkeep, and it soon became a crumbling heap that could not even keep out the wandering animals.

oh my

Stuyvesant tried to raise money to repair the wall, but he was unsuccessful. Today he would marvel at how important Wall Street has become not only to New York City, but to the entire world as well. He also would be astounded to see Manhattan today — the honking cars, buildings reaching to the sky, and crowds of people rushing by. But Peter Stuyvesant would still be able to find his way home.

New York: A Tory Refuge

BY CRAIG E. BLOHM

> New York had always been a politically turbulent city, and by the 1760s it was a center of revolutionary activity.

The stillness of a peaceful spring day in 1524 was abruptly shattered by the raucous shouts of sailors and the clatter of an anchor chain. The French ship *Dauphine,* commanded by Italian explorer Giovanni da Verrazano, had lowered its anchor into the water that would one day be called New York Bay. Verrazano, the first European to see New York, could not envision the bridges and skyscrapers of the great city that would one day rise upon the shore before him. Nor could he imagine the important role New York would play in the founding of the United States.

Not until eighty-five years later would another explorer's ship return to New York Bay. In 1609, Henry Hudson sailed his *Half Moon* up a river the Indians called Shatemuc (and we now know as the Hudson). Cruising up and down the river for several weeks, Hudson noted the area's wealth of natural resources. The English explorer reported back to his Dutch employers, and before long other expeditions followed. In 1624, the territory began a new life as New Netherland, and New York City was founded as New Amsterdam, a windmill towering over its fort.

England, however, still felt she had a claim on the territory. This was based on a voyage made by John Cabot in 1497, on which he sighted the coast of America and claimed the land for England. In 1664, King Charles II of England decided to make good Cabot's claim, so he gave New Netherland to his

6

brother James, duke of York and Albany. Four English warships sailed into the harbor in case the Dutch resisted the takeover. But on September 8, 1664, the colony surrendered without a fight. Overnight, New Netherland became New York.

New York had always been a politically turbulent city, and by the 1760s it was a center of revolutionary activity. Patriots in New York even staged their own "tea party" in April 1774, dumping English tea into the harbor as patriots in Boston had done the year before. The Tories, or Loyalists, who lived in the city increasingly became the targets of patriot attacks. Many who professed allegiance to the British Crown were jailed or beaten, while others left the city for safer areas. As 1776 began, New York City was in patriot hands, but history, and the British army, were about to change that.

In March 1776, General William Howe's British forces were driven from Boston by patriot artillery. Regrouping in Nova Scotia, Howe decided on New York for his next campaign. It was a logical choice, for New York stood midway between the New England and southern colonies. If Howe could capture the city, he could split the colonies and perhaps win the war. With thirty-two thousand men, Howe began his attack on New York. Long Island fell first, as Washington's inexperienced troops retreated from Howe's advance. By the fall of 1776, the American forces had fled, along with most of the civilian patriots.

Even before the Revolution, New York had more Loyalists than any other colony. This held true for New York City as well. One reason for this was the city's geographic location. Its strategic importance as a British military base, as well as its status as a seaport, provided close ties to the homeland. The British troops located in the city also were a factor, for soldiers needed to be housed and fed, and thus were a boon to business. Now that New York was controlled by the British, it became a haven for Loyalists from other areas of New York, as well as from Connecticut and New Jersey. When Howe's forces took over, about five thousand people remained in New York. By February 1777, the city's population had more than doubled, swelling to more than eleven thousand. (At the war's end, New York would have more than thirty thousand inhabitants.) Shortages in housing and food soon occurred across the city.

Rents increased fourfold, and water and fuel were in short supply. Adding to the problems for the refugee Tories was the fact that one-fourth of the city had been destroyed by a fire in September 1776. Despite the hardships, however, New York's Loyalists were safe from patriot persecution, and many businessmen even prospered.

There is probably no "typical" Tory, for loyalty to the Crown during the war crossed many social lines. In New York, many merchants and shopkeepers were Tories, for they stood to gain financially from the British. Some of these businessmen formerly had been Whigs favoring the patriot cause, but they had switched to the Loyalist camp out of economic necessity. Their business dealings with the English both in New York and across the ocean reminded them who their best customers were. In addition, many were heavily indebted to English creditors. Doctors and lawyers also tended to be Loyalists, as did some clergymen, especially those of the Anglican Church.

Some Tories supplemented their words with actions and joined the British army. Others aided the war effort by distributing counterfeit money, a ploy to wreck the Colonial economy. In June 1776, a group of Tories hatched a plot to kidnap George Washington and other Colonial leaders (see "The Plot to Kidnap Washington," pages 9–11). When the plan was discovered, those arrested included the mayor of New York and several of Washington's own bodyguards. But the Tories never played a major military role in the Revolution, for they were, by and large, ignored by the British government. Then, too, not all who favored the British cause were active; about one-third of New York's merchants remained neutral.

It was, perhaps, inevitable that a determined young America would win her independence. Just as British troops had entered New York City in 1776, in late 1783 they departed. With them went thousands of Loyalists who had made New York their home during the war. Many were exiled to Canada, others to West Indian islands. They left behind a city ravaged by war, her buildings gutted by fire and her streets ruined by neglect. Yet it was not the end but a new beginning for the city that would become one of America's greatest.

The Plot to Kidnap Washington

BY VIRGINIA CALKINS

I n the early summer of 1776, the Continental Congress was meeting in Philadelphia, planning to declare the independence of the American Colonies. At the same time, a group of Loyalists in New York was making daring plans of its own.

William Tryon, the royal governor of New York, was the leader of the group. When General George Washington made New York City his headquarters, Tryon moved to a ship, the HMS *Duchess of Gordon,* anchored just off the coast. From the ship, Tryon directed a system of spies and secret messengers that flourished among New York City's Loyalist population. Even the mayor, David Matthews, was a Loyalist. He had contributed one hundred pounds toward the plotters' expenses.

Gilbert Forbes, a gunsmith who had a shop on Broadway, was a member of the group. Governor Tryon would send money to Forbes, and he would use it to recruit men to join the British. Several members of Washington's own guard were corrupted in this way. An important part of the plan was the kidnapping of George Washington and members of his guard.

Hundreds of Loyalists intended to rise up and attack the American forces from the rear while the British army under General William Howe and the British navy under Admiral Richard Howe attacked the American front. The Loyalists were waiting impatiently for the Howe brothers to arrive with their troops.

Suddenly, things began to fall apart. It started when a couple of Loyalists were thrown into jail on a minor charge. They discussed the plot and were overheard by a man named Isaac Ketcham, who had been jailed for counterfeiting. He immediately realized that he had a golden opportunity to get himself out of trouble.

Ketcham sent a petition to the Provincial Congress, begging to be released on bail so he could take care of his six children. He added a little note to the speaker of the Provincial Congress in which he hinted that he had information on "another subject."

The speaker got the hint. He had Ketcham released long enough to have a private interview with him and make a deal. If Ketcham would do a little spying for the Americans, the charges against him would be dropped.

Back to prison went Ketcham. Soon he had two new cellmates, both of whom were charged with passing counterfeit money. They were Sergeant Thomas Hickey and Private Michael Lynch, members of Washington's guard. Ketcham pretended to be a Loyalist, and soon Hickey and Lynch were bragging to him about the clever plot in which they were involved. Ketcham sent a message to the Provincial Congress about what he had learned. The members had just heard the same

story from another source and alerted the army.

The Americans went into action. At one o'clock on the morning of June 22, Mayor David Matthews was arrested at his home in Flatbush. Gilbert Forbes was also arrested at about the same time. Other Tories were seized, but many escaped.

Hickey and Lynch, of course, were already behind bars, and the Americans decided to make an example of Thomas Hickey. On June 26, he went before a general court-martial. Several of the other plotters testified against him in exchange for immunity (protection from prosecution). Isaac Ketcham also testified.

Hickey had little to say in his own defense. At first he said that he "wanted to get some money out of the Tories." Then he said that he was afraid the British would take over, and if that happened, he wanted his name on record as being on their side. These remarks did not help Hickey's case, and the court-martial unanimously sentenced him to be hanged.

The next day a council of seven officers confirmed the sentence. George Washington himself presided. The

same today jailhouse snitch

council fixed the time of execution at eleven o'clock the next morning, June 28. The execution took place near the Bowery; it is said that twenty thousand people witnessed Hickey's hanging.

What happened to the other Loyalists involved in the plot? Governor Tryon continued to help the British and led troops that ravaged towns in Connecticut. In 1780, he moved to England. Mayor Matthews was sent as a prisoner to Governor Jonathan Trumbull in Hartford, Connecticut. He was charged with "treasonable practices against the states of America." After several months, he escaped and returned to New York, still claiming he was innocent. After the war, he moved to Canada.

The Loyalist plot was discovered just in the nick of time. On June 30, 1776, a British army under General William Howe landed on Staten Island. Two weeks later, his brother arrived with more troops. Washington and his army had to withdraw from New York, but at least the danger of a Loyalist attack from the rear had been removed.

The story of the Loyalist plot spread throughout the Colonies, being exaggerated as it spread. It served to intensify the hostility between the Loyalists and the fighters for independence.

Washington was quiet and calm about the whole episode. His main concern seemed to be the discipline of his troops.

The First Presidential Inauguration

BY KATHLEEN BURKE

About ten o'clock," wrote George Washington in his journal, "I bade adieu to Mt. Vernon." In mid-April 1789, he set out on an extraordinary journey. Six years had passed since the war had ended; Washington had returned eagerly to life on his Virginia estate. Now he was leaving his beloved home on the Potomac River. He set off for New York, where he would serve as his country's first president.

As Washington reached the outskirts of Alexandria, Virginia, his first stop along the way, friends and neighbors gathered to wish him well. From then on, in every village and city that Washington entered, crowds gathered to cheer the great war hero on his way. His passage north became a celebration of everyone's hopes for the new, young country.

As Washington approached Philadelphia, the governor of Pennsylvania and a cavalcade (ceremonial procession) of soldiers rode out to greet him. Crowds assembled along the roadside, hoping to catch even a glimpse of their distinguished countryman. One newspaper reported his arrival: "His EXCELLENCY rode in front of the procession, on horseback. The number of spectators who filled the doors, windows and streets...was greater than on any other occasion we ever remember. The joy of the whole city...cannot easily be described. Every countenance seemed to say, Long live GEORGE WASHINGTON, THE FATHER OF THE PEOPLE!"

In his oath of office, George Washington promised "to faithfully execute" the duties of the presidency.

As he approached Trenton, Washington entered a New Jersey region where he was especially loved. Here he had turned the British back in a decisive battle. As he crossed a bridge into the town, the famous general passed under a triumphal arch, woven of laurel leaves and flowers. Young girls scattered blossoms in his path, singing a refrain written for the occasion: "Welcome, mighty Chief! once more, Welcome to this grateful shore." This scene, recalled one witness, "was truly grand."

After six days' travel, Washington reached the New Jersey shore: New York lay just across the way. He embarked for the city on a special barge rowed by thirteen oarsmen — one for each of the original states.

The scene in New York Harbor was a splendid one indeed. Under a brilliant April sky, dozens of vessels formed a great nautical procession. Washington recalled the spectacle — "the display of boats, the decorations of the ships, the roar of the cannon, the loud acclamations of the people...as I passed along the wharves" — in his journal that evening.

At mid-afternoon, Washington disembarked at the foot of Wall Street. Enormous crowds waited along his route. Everywhere he passed, people leaned from windows and rained flowers on his head. The entire city joined in the festivities.

No room was to be found in any lodging house. People set up tents wherever they could find a place; some even slept in the streets. Whatever the hardships, though, no one seemed to mind. As one girl wrote to her family in Boston: "I have seen him!... I should have known at a glance that it was General Washington; I never saw a human being that looked so grand and noble.... I could fall down on my knees before him and bless him for all the good he has done for this country."

At last, one week later, the event everyone had awaited arrived — Washington's inauguration day, April 30, 1789. Church bells rang out across New York. At noon, the parade began. The president-elect traveled in a gleaming, cream-colored carriage, accompanied by an escort of guardsmen elegant in blue coats and white breeches; foot soldiers marching in step; statesmen who would attend the swearing-in; and distinguished citizens. Cheering spectators lined the route.

The procession wound through

the streets to the newly refurbished Federal State House on Wall Street. Washington entered the marble vestibule and crossed into the Senate chamber. From that room, he stepped out to a balcony. The expectant crowd, stretching as far as he could see, broke into a great cheer at his sight. Washington placed his hand over his heart and bowed to his countrymen.

Then a hush fell over everyone. Resplendent in his dark brown coat and breeches, his dress sword, and his silver-buckled shoes, Washington turned to take the oath of office. Laying his hand on the Bible, he promised "to faithfully execute" the duties of the presidency. He concluded with the words, "I swear, so help me God." Hurrahs rang out again, as a thirteen-gun salute greeted the new president.

As the brief ceremony ended, Washington returned to the Senate chamber and addressed both houses of Congress. As he spoke about "the great experiment entrusted to the American people," he seemed deeply conscious of his new responsibilities. The new president expressed his own fears at the great task that lay before him. One senator recorded his memory of Washington's "aspect grave, almost to sadness, his modesty...his voice deep, a little tremulous, and so low as to call for close attention." The speech, he reported, "produced emotion of the most affecting kind upon the members."

That evening was marked by even more dramatic festivities. Candles glowed in the windows of every house and shone from every ship in the harbor. Crowds gathered at the lower end of the city to watch a two-hour fireworks display. "We returned home on foot," wrote one spectator in his journal, "the throng of people being so great as not to permit a carriage to pass through it." It was a young nation's historic celebration, never to be forgotten by those who witnessed this inauguration of their country's first president.

'THE HARDEST VOLUNTEER JOB'

BY CAROL G. TRAUB

The term "First Lady" was coined by newspaperwoman Mary Clemmer Ames in 1877. It has since become the accepted unofficial title for the wife of the president of the United States.

Martha Washington hosts a reception in New York City during her husband's presidency.

The role of First Lady is not mentioned in the Constitution, and there is no job description. The First Lady is neither elected nor paid, yet her undefined but demanding role has been called "the hardest volunteer job" in the world. Through the years of our country's history, First Ladies have filled this role in many ways, each true to her own unique personality.

In 1789, when Martha Washington arrived in New York, the temporary capital, she did not have the example of a previous First Lady to follow and had to establish a role for herself. As was typical of women of her day, she continued to act as homemaker and hostess for her husband, but her parties were stiff and formal. This was not entirely Martha's fault. The president and his advisors were so anxious to make the new government appear in every way legitimate in the eyes of the world that they patterned their social events on those of the European courts.

As "Lady Washington," Martha remained seated and received her guests while her husband mingled. She ended the parties at nine o'clock by announcing that it was "the General's bedtime." Her social events were sometimes criticized by the president's political opponents, prompting her to write to a friend that the role was "better suited to younger and gayer women."

National Capital to Financial Capital

BY DUANE DAMON

For a spring afternoon in New York City, the weather was fair. People had been pouring into the nation's capital for days, and the crowd outside Federal Hall was restless, expectant.

On the balcony above them, a tall man gravely stepped to the low iron railing. His graying reddish hair was powdered a snowy white. His suit was cut from brown broadcloth made in Connecticut. The man placed his right hand on a Bible resting on a crimson cushion. Robert R. Livingston, chancellor of the State of New York, administered the oath.

"I solemnly swear," repeated George Washington, "that I will faithfully execute the office of the President of the United States, and will, to the best of my ability, preserve, protect and defend the Constitution of the United States." He bent to kiss the Bible.

Livingston turned to the crowd and said, "Long live George Washington, President of the United States!" The crowd, spilling out of Wall Street and down Broad, roared its approval. Church bells across town tolled their own tribute. Southward on the Battery, the thunder of cannon resounded. This celebration was not New York's alone.

On this first Inauguration Day, April 30, 1789, the eyes of the entire republic were on the city.

Nestled at the lower end of Manhattan Island, New York was the political center of the country. Since 1785, the federal Congress had met in the old City Hall building, now called Federal Hall.

The city also boasted an endless variety of businesses. Coach makers, booksellers, wine dealers, and pewterers competed with wig makers, farriers, and two daily newspapers for shoppers' money. For liquid refreshment, a visitor could stop at any of the 169 taverns and public houses. To refresh his spirit, he had his choice of twenty-two churches. While there were no hospitals, doctors and dentists were plentiful, as were lawyers.

Wall Street, shown here as it appeared in the 1790s, has been a center of business activity ever since.

The heart of much of this activity was Wall Street. Here was located the Bank of New York, which had opened in 1784, and the newly renovated Federal Hall. The Post Office was not far away. At 58 Wall Street stood the law office of Alexander Hamilton. Lining the west end of the street were some of the largest and most elegant houses in New York. The homes and offices of merchants and bankers stood on the street, making it one of the country's major commercial centers.

But changes were coming. As secretary of the treasury, Hamilton proposed that the federal government take on the staggering burden of the states' war debts. To win southern support, Hamilton dangled a tempting carrot in front of the South's lawmakers. In 1790, the capital would be moved from New York to a temporary home in Philadelphia. After ten years, it would shift to a permanent southern site on the Potomac River.

New York's loss would be Wall Street's gain. Eighty million dollars in government bonds were sold to pay off the war debt, and New York's thriving trade gave the city ample money for investing. This made it an excellent market for the resale of the new government securities. Before long, the sidewalks of Wall Street were humming with a huge trade in federal bonds.

In 1792, Hamilton established the first federal bank, and shares of the bank's stock were offered to the public. As financial trade grew, a group of men joined together to organize an association of brokers on Wall Street. From that grew the New York Stock and Exchange Board, which was founded in 1817. In 1793, the Tontine Coffee House was built on the corner of Wall and Water streets. It was not just an inn but an important meeting place for businessmen and the first official headquarters of the brokers group.

Geography was a major factor in New York's success. Its harbor was the largest and finest on the North Atlantic. Its central location made the city the crucial link between the vast raw materials of the United States and the powerful industries of Britain. New York's waterways also brought the city within easy reach of profitable markets such as upstate New York and southern New England.

If New York provided the spirit, Wall Street furnished the cash. Its bustling stock exchange and independent brokers sold state and private bonds to finance roads, bridges, and canals. As New York grew, trading on Wall Street grew with it.

In 1800, sixty thousand residents made New York the most populous city in the nation. That number swelled to half a million by mid-century. When a devastating fire swept through lower Manhattan in 1835, more than seven hundred buildings were destroyed. Wall Street joined its neighbors in the cleanup and rebuilding that followed, replacing many wooden homes that had been destroyed with office buildings. By the late 1860s, New York was erecting several hundred buildings each year.

As the city grew, Manhattan's fashionable district shifted northward. Upper-class residents moved uptown, and expensive hotels, stores, and other retail establishments followed. Some of the houses left behind were torn down, and others were renovated.

By 1870, Wall Street was no longer an avenue of fancy shops and fine houses. It had become a street of investment banks and brokerages. Five- and six-story buildings of brick or stone had replaced the low, Federal-style wood structures of Washington's day. In 1865, the New York Stock Exchange had taken up quarters just next door on Broad Street, but it was still referred to as being "on Wall Street." As Wall Street's importance as a financial center grew, its name came to mean not just the street itself but the entire financial district of New York.

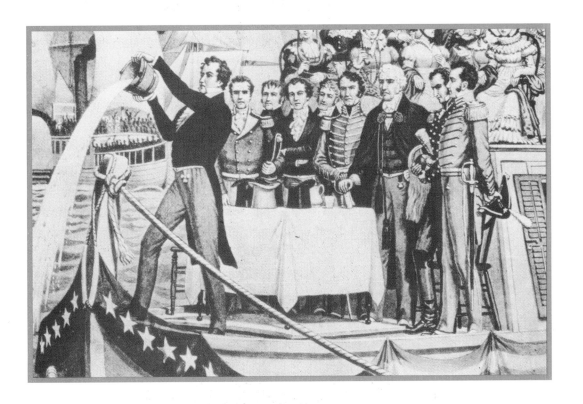

Marriage of the Waters

BY PEG CONNOLLY SCHWABEL

The morning of October 26, 1825, was a satisfying one for New York State's governor, DeWitt Clinton. His dream had been fulfilled. The canal across New York State that he had worked and planned for was finally finished. Now Clinton, together with other Americans, was ready to celebrate.

Above: New York governor DeWitt Clinton pours Lake Erie water into the Atlantic Ocean in the "Marriage of the Waters" ceremony.

A brass band led the parade that moved from the New York courthouse in Buffalo to the edge of the newly completed canal. Buffalo was on the western end of the canal, and Governor Clinton was prepared to make the first official trip along the full length of the waterway. He would travel to Albany, New York, on the canal boat *Seneca Chief,* colorfully decorated for the occasion.

Plans for the celebration in honor of the opening of the canal had been discussed for weeks. Some people even called the waterway the Eighth Wonder of the World. The Erie Canal would provide quick, cheap transportation to the West. Through the canal, the waters of the Atlantic were joined with the waters of the Great Lakes. Citizens and government officials were so pleased with this that they planned a special ceremony, one they called the "Marriage of the Waters."

At 10 A.M., Buffalo militiamen fired a large cannon as Governor Clinton stepped onto the *Seneca Chief.* Then, pulled by a team of horses, the canal boat began to move east. Behind the *Seneca Chief,* four other canal boats took their positions. There were cheers and salutes everywhere.

News of the events at Buffalo was sent to citizens across the state in a very special manner. Cannon had been placed approximately ten miles apart along the route of the canal and along the Hudson River to New York City. The cannon served as a kind of message relay system. When the people manning the cannon ten miles east of Buffalo heard the shot that was fired as Governor Clinton stepped onto the *Seneca Chief,* they fired their cannon. This was heard by the people at the cannon ten miles farther east, and the message was relayed in this manner all the way across the state. By 11:30 A.M., news of Governor Clinton's departure had reached New York City.

As Clinton and his party passed through the towns and villages along the canal, they were greeted by fireworks, banquets, and parades. Everyone was curious about the two colorfully painted kegs on the deck of the *Seneca Chief.* These kegs, decorated with a painting of an eagle and with the words "The Waters of Lake Erie," were to be a part of the "marriage" celebration in New York City.

Behind the *Seneca Chief,* the canal boat *Noah's Ark* carried two Seneca Indian boys, a bear, a beaver, two eagles, and various birds and fish. These were all symbols of the West before the coming of settlers and were an important part of the celebration.

On November 2, seven days after the start of its journey, the *Seneca Chief* passed from the Erie Canal into the Hudson River. Eight steamboats took the canal boats in tow and, on November 4, 1825, the boats from Buffalo reached New York Harbor.

Cannon from New York City's forts were fired in celebration. Dozens of boats with whistles and cheering passengers gathered around the smaller canal boats. Then, in a grand water parade, the *Seneca Chief* was towed by the steamboat *Washington* to Sandy Hook where the waters of New York Harbor flow into the Atlantic Ocean.

At last, to highlight the New York celebration, Governor Clinton performed the "marriage." Slowly, he poured the kegs of Lake Erie water into the Atlantic. Then, to honor the occasion in another way, a mixture of water from the Rhine, the Amazon, and nine other major rivers from around the world was added to those of the Atlantic and the Great Lakes. This act symbolized the fact that products from all parts of the world could now be carried to the American West.

When Governor Clinton and his guests returned to New York City, they were greeted by the biggest celebration in the history of the city. A parade five miles long marched through the streets. Later that night, three thousand people attended an elegant ball in honor of the canal. It was the largest ball ever held in the United States up to that time.

Yet one final ceremony to honor the opening of the Erie Canal remained — water from the Atlantic had to be poured into Lake Erie. The *Seneca Chief* returned to Buffalo with a keg of Atlantic water, and on November 25 this water was added to Lake Erie, completing the world's most unusual "wedding" ceremony.

One year later, nineteen thousand boats and forty thousand settlers had used the Erie Canal to go west. New York City had become a major seaport, and Buffalo was becoming a major trade center. Everyone agreed that the marriage of Lake Erie to the Atlantic was a success.

An American Folksong

INTRODUCTION BY
ROSALIND SCHILDER

Folksongs are stories set to music. The first ones were created long before the printing press was invented. They were passed on orally from person to person, from place to place, and from one generation to the next. Every country has its own special types of folksongs that are composed not by professional musicians but by common folk. These songs tell about the joys, sorrows, hopes, and despair of people all over the world and of times past and present. The most famous Erie Canal folksong, "Low Bridge, Everybody Down," or "Fifteen Miles on the Erie Canal," is a good example.

Life on the canal was slow, quiet, and often monotonous. Yet many of the songs that have come down to us about that waterway are full of high adventure and heroic feats. These songs were made up by canal boat crews. The songs helped them to pass the time, to amuse each other, and to avoid falling asleep on night trips. Different versions of this Erie Canal folksong have been found in Texas, Illinois, Washington, Montana, New York, and Pennsylvania. In some versions, Sal was a mule who pulled the boat. In others, she was the cook. In other versions, Sal was described as "cross-eyed Sal," "as handsome as a pig," "freckled and twenty-three," "redheaded and sixty-three," and "Big-foot Sal."

But the most popular rendition of the song tells us of life on the Erie Canal as it really was — slow, steady-paced, and monotonous — and of Sal, a companion who bore her share of the burden. The words and the music to this popular version appear here. You can play it on the piano or ask someone else to do it and sing along.

Low Bridge, Everybody Down

STEPS IN TIME:
STARTING A NATION
• • • • • • • • • • • • • • • • • • • •
BY BETTY H. LITTLE

Find the events that relate especially to New York City,
then put them together to make your own New York City time line.

1776   Declaration of Independence signed.

1780s   Philadelphia, Pennsylvania; Princeton, New Jersey; Trenton, New Jersey; Annapolis, Maryland; and New York City take turns being United States capital.

1781   Articles of Confederation adopted (March 1).

1782   United States and Great Britain begin peace talks.

1783   Peace of Versailles (also called Treaty of Paris) signed (September 3); Noah Webster publishes *Blue-Backed Speller.*

1784   Phillis Wheatley, first important black American poet, dies.

1785   Land Ordinance provides for survey of Northwest Territory.

1787   Northwest Ordinance enacted; Constitutional Convention meets; Washington elected president of Constitutional Convention (May 25).

1787–1788 *The Federalist Papers* published.

1788   United States Constitution ratified; New York City becomes federal capital.

1789   George Washington elected first president; first federal Congress meets.

1790   Philadelphia becomes federal capital; first United States census — 3,929,214; President Washington approves plans for Washington, D.C., as federal capital; Ben Franklin dies.

1800   Washington, D.C., becomes the permanent United States capital.

BOOKS TO READ

George and Martha Washington at Home in New York *by Beatrice Siegel* (Chicago: Childrens Press, 1989) describes the life the Washingtons shared when New York City was the country's capital. Includes a map of the city in 1789. Grade 4 and up.

A Historical Album of New York *by Monique Avakian and Carter Smith III* (Brookfield, Connecticut: The Millbrook Press, 1993) follows the history of New York State and New York City from pre-Colonial times to the present. Grade 4 and up.

New York *by Bruce Glassman* (Woodbridge, Connecticut: Blackbirch Press, 1991) is divided into three sections: an introduction to New York, the city's history, and the people who live there. Grade 3 and up.

New York City *by Barbara Johnston Adams* (Parsippany, New Jersey: Silver Burdett Press, 1996) includes a historical time line, a list of places to visit, and pictures to provide both past and present views of New York City. Grade 3 and up.

MORE MEDIA

The Big Apple. This award-winning video produced by the Museum of the City of New York uses the museum's collection to tell a story of the city spanning more than three hundred years. Contact museum: (212) 534-1672.

The Big Apple Movie. This video from New York City's visitors center introduces the city to tourists. It includes information about famous places in New York and clips from movies filmed in the city. Contact Visitors Bureau: (212) 397-8222.

PLACES TO VISIT

Museum of the City of New York. This museum tells the history of the city through its large collection of objects from life in New Amsterdam to New York today.

National Museum of the American Indian. Information about Native Americans from all regions of the country is presented in this large museum.

Battery Park. The park, with views of the harbor and the Statue of Liberty, is at the southern tip of Manhattan, not far from the original Fort Amsterdam built by the Dutch. You can tour Castle Clinton, a fort built in 1811.

South Street Seaport. Buildings from the 1800s form the center of this preserved neighborhood on the city's waterfront. There is also a museum about New York's history as a port city.

2 Building the City

NEW YORK CITY IS MORE THAN THREE HUNDRED YEARS OLD. YOU can visit places here that go back farther than the founding of our country and places that look ahead to the future.

Take a tour of New York then and now to see how our city was built. The New York City of today was not actually created until 1898, when the five boroughs — Manhattan, the Bronx, Brooklyn, Queens, and Staten Island — united to form one of the world's largest cities. You will visit each of the five boroughs.

Do you know how Harlem got its name? Did you ever wonder what SoHo means? You will find out the meaning of the names of these and many other places in our city.

What would New York be today without Central Park, the public libraries, and the Brooklyn Bridge? Used every day by thousands of people, these places help make this city a special place to live. But like so many places in New York, they also have a fascinating history.

Today we all take electricity for granted. Travel back to September 4, 1882, to watch Thomas Edison turn on electric bulbs in a New York office for the first time.

Ulysses S. Grant was an army general and president of the United States. In the early 1880s, Grant and his family settled in New York City. Here he wrote a book about his life that became a bestseller after he died. You can visit the huge tomb where Grant is buried.

There is even a museum with exhibits on the history of our city. The Museum of the City of New York has more than one million objects that were made, worn, or used by New Yorkers over the past three hundred years.

There are hundreds of other famous places to visit in New York. Take a tour of fabulous museums, watch leaders from around the world at the United Nations, and walk through historic sailing ships and a World War II aircraft carrier.

Are there really alligators living in New York's sewers? Find out how that story got started.

Finally, make your own time capsule in "History for the Future" on pages 60–61.

Five in One: The Boroughs of NYC

BY MARY ELLEN HEIDGEN AND SALLY PLACKSIN

n 1898, the boroughs (counties) of Manhattan, the Bronx, Brooklyn (Kings County), Queens, and Staten Island (Richmond County) united to form New York City. Connected by a series of bridges, tunnels, and far-reaching subway tracks, these five boroughs have many different characteristics. People who live in Manhattan refer to the other boroughs as "the outer boroughs," while outer-borough residents call Manhattan "the city."

Bronx

The Bronx is the northernmost borough and the only one that is on the U.S. mainland. It was named for the Danish landholder Jonas Bronck, who owned a farm here. A peninsula, the Bronx was once a shipping and warehouse center. Today it is home to ten universities, the New York Botanical Gardens, and the New York Zoological Park (the famous Bronx Zoo). Yankee Stadium, built in 1923, was the stadium in which Babe Ruth, Lou Gehrig, and Joe DiMaggio played.

Manhattan

New York City began in Manhattan in 1624, when the Dutch founded New Amsterdam in the area where the skyscrapers of the financial district are today. In the early 1600s, an English mapmaker learned some place names from the Indians who lived at the mouth of the Hudson River. The land to the east of the river was called Man-ahahtin, probably meaning "hilly island," which eventually evolved into Manhattan. Among Manhattan's varied attractions are its many bridges, museums, stores, restaurants, theaters, famous and historic places to visit, and unique neighborhoods.

Queens

Queens is the largest borough geographically, with more than two hundred miles of waterfront. It was named for Queen Catherine of Braganza, wife of the ruling English king, Charles II, in 1683. The Queens Museum (home to the Panorama of the City of New York, an architectural model of the city as it appears today) and the New York Hall of Science are located in Flushing Meadows Corona Park, on the site of the 1939–1940 and 1964–1965 world's fairs. The New York Mets baseball team plays here in Shea Stadium, and two large airports, John F. Kennedy International and La Guardia, are located here.

Brooklyn

Named by the Dutch after a town in the Netherlands (Breuckelen), Brooklyn evolved into the second most populous borough, consisting of many settlements and villages. It still has a reputation for its various and distinct neighborhoods. It is also famous for its many churches and universities, as well as Prospect Park, the site of a battle during the American Revolution, and Coney Island, an amusement park and home of the famous Coney Island hot dog. Aside from its neighborhoods, Brooklyn is known for its industry. Machinery, textiles, and paper products are manufactured here.

Staten Island

In 1609, English explorer Henry Hudson, who was employed by the Dutch, named this fourteen-mile-long island Staaten Eylandt, meaning "Island of the States." In 1664, the English formally renamed it Richmond County, to honor the English duke of Richmond, but it is still popularly known as Staten Island. Until the Verrazano-Narrows Bridge was built in 1964 connecting it to Brooklyn, the island remained somewhat rural, although some industry existed before then. The Staten Island Ferry, which travels from the Battery (lower Manhattan) to the island through New York Harbor, provides great views of the Statue of Liberty and Ellis Island.

What's in a Name?

BY SALLY PLACKSIN

"What's in a name?" the famous playwright William Shakespeare asked. Plenty, when it comes to teaching us more about the history of New York City! Broadway, Wall Street, and Manhattan are familiar names in New York today, but where did they come from?

Imagine that you could become a "word detective" and travel back in time to different years and neighborhoods around New York. You would be on the scene to discover firsthand where many names originated.

Suppose you went all the way back to the 1600s. You could take a walk along Beaver Street and see what was then just a narrow lane at the southern tip of Manhattan Island, where American Indians brought their beaver pelts to the Dutch ships that were anchored in the Hudson River. You could then zoom ahead a couple of centuries to the 1800s and take a walk through the newly opened Central Park, where sheep grazed peacefully in what is today called the Sheep Meadow. You could finish your day by visiting Harlem in the 1920s, where people came hoping to make "the big time," a term that has evolved into New York City's famous nickname, "the Big Apple."

Here are the stories of some more place names connected with New York's history and culture.

> Broadway, Wall Street, and Manhattan are familiar names in New York today, but where did they come from?

New Amsterdam

This Dutch town on the southern tip of Manhattan Island was an early settlement named for the famous city in the Netherlands. Although the town had one hundred twenty houses by 1656, the streets still had no names. Within two years, however, New Amsterdam had named streets, many of which described the landscape: Bridge Street, for example, was a street where a bridge stood.

New York

In 1664, Colonel Richard Nicolls arrived in New Amsterdam with an English fleet. The Dutch governor, Peter Stuyvesant, surrendered, and Nicolls renamed both New Netherland and New Amsterdam. He called them New York, in honor of the duke of York, the English king's brother.

Broadway

Long before we came to know this world-famous street as Broadway, it was an American Indian trail running north-south through the forest. This wide street was officially called Heere Straat, or "Lord's Street," by the Dutch and Great George Street by the English, but it was more commonly known as Breede Wegh, "Broad Way."

Wall Street

In 1653, the Dutch erected a fortification running across Manhattan Island to defend the city against an expected attack by English settlers from New England. The Dutch settlers called it De Waal. The wall was demolished in 1699, but its site became Wall Street, where the New York Stock Exchange now stands.

Ladies Mile

Ladies Mile was a shopping area that had its heyday following the Civil War. It was ten blocks long, running from Union Square (Fourteenth Street) to Madison Square (Twenty-third Street), and three blocks wide (from Broadway to Sixth Avenue). Lord & Taylor, FAO Schwartz, Brooks Brothers, and Tiffany & Co. were just a few of the stores found there. These stores offered shoppers something new — window-shopping! They had big plate-glass windows on the street level, showing grand displays of the merchandise to be found inside. In those days, women usually did not go out without a male escort, but they could go shopping by themselves.

Harlem

One of the world's most important

centers of African American life and culture, this section of the city was originally named Haarlem after a town in the Netherlands. The English later changed the spelling to Harlem. During the twentieth century, certain streets were given special names. Edgecombe Avenue above 145th Street became known as "Sugar Hill." It was considered a "sweet" place to live because it was home to many successful and creative African Americans from all walks of life.

The Dakota

When this enormous apartment building on Central Park West between Seventy-second and Seventy-third streets was built, it was so far from the downtown "center" of city life that it seemed as distant as the western plains of Dakota — and that's how it got its name! Today it is the home of many famous artists, actors, and musicians.

SoHo

SoHo is the name of an area of lower Manhattan that runs between Houston Street on the north and Canal Street on the south. It is short for "south of Houston (Street)." Once a neighborhood of factories where few people except struggling artists lived, this forty-block area has now become a lively center for musicians, filmmakers, writers, and visual and performance artists. Twenty-six of the blocks have been declared a historic district, where the nineteenth-century architecture and cobblestone streets will be preserved.

The Vision of Frederick Law Olmsted

BY MARNIE LAIRD

One hundred twenty-five years ago, the proposed site for Central Park in New York City presented a dismal picture. The 843 acres were swampy and brush-filled, with poor soil. Squatters' tumble-down shacks were eyesores, and debris littered the ground. Thousands of wild dogs and goats infested the area. The air stank from nearby slaughterhouses and hog farms.

Thanks to the vision of Frederick Law Olmsted, Central Park today ranks as one of the most beautiful and famous city parks in the world. Born in 1822 in Hartford, Connecticut, this strange and brilliant man came into a world where there were no public parks. But during his lifetime, he built many beautiful parks, because he believed that people need-ed green places to keep them healthy in both body and spirit.

By the time Olmsted was thirty-five years old, he was a jack of all trades and master of none. As a writer and journalist, he spoke out against slavery. Appointed by Abraham Lincoln to the Sanitary Commission during the Civil War, he laid the foundation for the American branch of the Red Cross. One hundred years before conservation became a worldwide issue, Olmsted was dedicated to preserving our environment. As a farmer, he combined gardening and engineering to create a new profession called landscape architecture.

It was through his use of landscape architecture that he changed the face of this country. The most attractive features of many cities

New York City's skyline has changed since Frederick Law Olmsted's time. Today Central Park is surrounded by skyscrapers and office buildings.

across the United States today are the parks that he designed.

Olmsted's work began in 1857. The Central Park commissioners declared a competition for a new plan for the future park. Calvert Vaux, a noted architect, asked Olmsted to join him in designing a plan for the competition. They were the perfect team: Vaux designed the buildings and bridges, and Olmsted concentrated on the landscape design. To ensure as much open space and rural atmosphere as possible, Olmsted conceived a brilliant plan for sinking the crosstown roads below ground into open cuts and tunnels, so that traffic would not intrude on the scenery. He designed lakes, nature walks, and recreation areas. The plan, named Greensward, won first prize.

Vaux considered the park a work of art, but Olmsted saw it in terms of people. The city was rapidly swelling with immigrants. Living in crowded, unhealthy tenements, these poor people had little access to green grass and fresh air. At a time when much of New York City was still undeveloped, Olmsted foresaw the vast metropolis it would someday become. He recognized the need for open space for its residents. He believed that natural surroundings were essential to the well-being of all people — an outlook shared by today's mental health experts.

Olmsted saw the park as a way to bring the rural countryside into the bustling city. With startling accuracy, Olmsted predicted in a speech delivered in 1858, "No longer an open suburb, Central Park will have around it a continuous high wall of brick, stone, and marble. The adjoining shore will be lined with commercial docks and warehouses. Steamboat and ferry landings, railroad stations, hotels, theaters, and factories will be on all sides of it, and above it, all of which our park must be made to fit."

The transformation of the existing swampland into the great park we know today was a monumental job. Olmsted was appointed supervisor of the entire park and commanded a crew of twenty-five hundred men. Sixty miles of pipe were laid to drain the swampy land. Two hundred sixty tons of gunpowder were used for blasting rocks and making reservoirs. Almost five million trees and shrubs were planted in a space stretching two and a half miles north and south and half a mile across.

Olmsted's vision of the city's growth and the walls of brick and stone came true. Today the seven million people living in New York love their park, and thousands use it every day.

Central Park made Olmsted world famous. He proceeded to design Brooklyn and Prospect Parks in Brooklyn, as well as Morningside and Riverside Drives in Manhattan, Mont Royal Park in Montreal, and Jackson Park in Chicago. In Boston, he planned a regional park system that became a necklace of green space surrounding the city.

Olmsted also designed the grounds of the United States Capitol in Washington, D.C. He created open spaces, shaded walkways, and vistas on one side and planned an impressive marble terrace to surround the rest of the huge building. Foreseeing the "suburban commuter towns" of today, where many city workers live, he created plans for communities to protect the beauty of the existing landscape.

When asked by the City of San Francisco to submit a plan for a great park, Olmsted designed a remarkable plan that would reduce damage caused by earthquakes and fires. He proposed a sunken parkway that would also serve as a firebreak. Had the city adopted his plan, the parkway would have helped to control the city's terrible fire caused by the 1906 earthquake. Ironically, the fire was finally checked by dynamiting houses along the very site of his proposed parkway.

Olmsted's vision of parks for people spread across the United States. He encouraged the federal government to involve itself in the creation of national recreation areas. The seeds of environmental awareness he was planting would one day bear fruit as the National Park system.

Olmsted remained active in landscape design until his death at age eighty-one in 1903. Even though he had left school at age fourteen, both Harvard and Yale awarded him honorary degrees. By the end of his life, Olmsted's dream, to preserve open space for future Americans, had been realized in projects throughout the country and in Canada.

CENTRAL PARK

BY JOHN J. BONK

Whisk me away to a tree-covered
   world and surround me with nothing but green.
Squawking ducks in a lake, and long
   walks we could take,
Where the air is all dewy and clean.

Pack up a lunch and we'll picnic till
   dusk on a hill overlooking a stream.
In the distance the sound of a merry-
   go-round.
Faces covered with smiles and ice
   cream.

Kick off your shoes and we'll tickle our
   toes as we frolic through crispy tall
   grass.
Then we'll rest for a bit, find a nice
   bench and sit,
As we watch all the passersby pass.

Horses clop by pulling tourist-filled
carriages driven by men in top hats.
Sweethearts stroll hand in hand
toward the souvenir stand.
Muddy kids lug their baseballs and
bats.

Roughnecks on skateboards, and
babies in buggies, and grandmothers having long talks.
Joggers jog, hikers hike, skaters skate,
bikers bike,
Barking dogs take their owners for
walks.

Artists at easels are capturing scenery,
sunbathers soak up the sun.
Little children aglow at a free puppet
show,
Crowds are cheering a marathon run.

People applaud for a man with a saxo-
phone playing a medley of tunes.
Toss some coins in his case, watch it
light up his face,
And we'll spend all the rest on
balloons.

Faraway skyscrapers seem to be
stretching their necks for a peek in
the park.
They pop over the trees just as if to
say, "Please,
Hurry home now before it gets dark!"

Riders on horseback head back to the
stables, and bird watchers call it a
day.
Games of chess disappear as the
evening grows near.
Hot dog vendors are rolling away.

Wait, not so fast! There are still things
to see like an outdoor Shakespeare-
an play.
There are concerts at night under
stars and moonlight,
Ending under a fireworks display.

Shaking the ground comes a rumbling
of thunder, and lightning is piercing
the sky.
Grab your stuff! Better run! We've had
nothing but fun.
But for now, Central Park, it's
good-bye!

The Eighth Wonder of the World

BY ELLEN HARDSOG

On the hot, humid afternoon of August 25, 1876, a crowd of thousands lined the banks of New York's East River. Men in damp shirtsleeves and women in wide-brimmed hats raised their eyes to a spot 276 feet above the water, where a flagman waited atop the tower of a yet unfinished bridge. Suddenly, the red signal flag moved against the sky. The watchers strained their eyes to see a tiny chair traveling the narrow steel cable that joined the tower to its twin near the New York shore.

As the dangling seat inched its way across the river, the passenger, Master Mechanic E.F. Farrington, merrily waved his straw hat. The spectators cheered, and from the boat-filled river rose a deafening fanfare of horns and whistles. All of Brooklyn and New York applauded the first person to cross the fabulous Brooklyn Bridge.

The Great Bridge, as it was known, had been designed in 1857 by a German immigrant and bridge builder named John Roebling. Roebling wished to solve the problem of undependable commuter ferry service between Brooklyn and New York. City officials, hoping the bridge would make Brooklyn important, accepted the plan and formed a company to pay for it. But before construction could begin, John Roebling lost his toes in an accident at the ferry landing and died of tetanus soon after.

Roebling's oldest son then took up his father's dream. A talented engineer, Washington Roebling borrowed ideas from European and American bridges. But because the Brooklyn Bridge

Fireworks light up the Brooklyn Bridge during its one hundredth anniversary celebration in 1983.

would be like no other bridge before it, the young man invented many new techniques of his own. The bridge would be half again as long as any other, with a roadway for carriages and cable cars and a unique promenade where people could stroll across the river. For the first time, steel cables would be used instead of cast iron. The bridge's towers would dwarf all buildings on either side of the river, and the roadway would be built 135 feet above the river to permit tall clipper ships to pass beneath. It would be, by far, the grandest and boldest bridge ever built, and a symbol of America's proud spirit.

Construction began in 1869. To support the massive towers, two open-bottomed wooden caissons were constructed, towed into position, and sunk into the river bottom. Each caisson, 168 by 102 feet, had six chambers, which were filled with compressed air. Into the chambers went workmen to dig out the rock and earth below the caissons. Huge granite blocks that were to be part of the towers stood atop the caissons and drove them down from above.

Working conditions were horrible. The heavy air pressure, the slimy mud, the sounds of groaning men and chipping pickaxes, and the eerie light of candles and calcium lamps were shocking to reporters and visitors who entered the caissons. Many of the laborers were German, Irish, and Italian immigrants. They worked for two or three dollars a day in three shifts.

By the time Roebling was satisfied that the caissons were firmly settled and ready to be filled with concrete, several problems had begun to hamper the project. A fire in the Brooklyn caisson in December 1879 burned deep into the timbers and later forced the reconstruction of part of the caisson's roof. As the caissons were pushed downward, the air pressure inside had to be raised. This caused a strange illness among the workers called caisson disease, or "the bends." After leaving the caisson's compressed air, many workers collapsed with painful cramps and paralysis. Some never completely recovered, and, worse, a few died. Little was known then about the cause of the

bends, a disease suffered by people who move rapidly from the high-pressure environment of the deep sea to the ordinary pressure at the surface. Washington Roebling fell ill with caisson disease so often that he was forced to spend the final ten years of the project observing the work from his bedroom window. He watched through binoculars and wrote down detailed instructions, which his wife, Emily, took regularly to the construction site.

In spite of these obstacles, by the summer of 1876 the great towers were finished and the cable spinning had begun. The four main cables were formed of 3,515 miles of wire. Single wires were spun into strands, with nineteen strands in turn bound high above the river into cables 16 inches in diameter.

After fourteen years and sixteen million dollars, the Brooklyn Bridge was completed and opened on May 24, 1883. President Chester Arthur led the opening day parade. The newspapers called the bridge the "Eighth Wonder of the World," and even after one hundred years, Americans still marvel at its unique design and beauty.

Let There Be Light

BY BRUCE WATSON

A t a quarter to three on September 4, 1882, Thomas Edison set out on foot through the streets of lower Manhattan. Horses and buggies jammed Pearl Street, and a snarl of telegraph wires blocked the sky. No one paid much attention to the inventor in the frock coat and white derby as he walked toward his appointment with the future.

Turning onto Wall Street, Edison wondered if he had dared too much this time. At 3 P.M., his assistant would throw the switch at Pearl Street station. The huge dynamos (generators) would send a sizzling current through copper rods laid beneath the streets. If the plan worked, electric bulbs would blaze all over the business district of New York City. If it failed, or if a circuit

> *"We will make electric light so cheap that only the rich will be able to burn candles."*

box blew and power leaked into the street, what city would give him another chance?

Just before three, Edison reached the office of Drexel, Morgan and Company. His dark hair was a mess; his hands were greasy from last-minute work. Several men in silk hats and tweed suits, who had invested six hundred thousand dollars in Edison's dream, met him at the door. Was everything finally ready? Would it work?

As the clock's hands swept toward three, a crowd gathered around the inventor in the plush office. Edison moved to the main switch. At the back of the room, a skeptic shouted, "A hundred dollars says the bulbs don't work."

"Taken!" Edison said and

reached for the light.

Until the 1880s, U.S. cities were lit by gas lamps. Whether kerosene or natural gas, the lamps burned dimly but cost little. Although Edison had become famous after his invention of the incandescent bulb in 1879, when he announced his plan to light up New York, people scoffed. Never mind that the "Wizard of Menlo Park" had already invented the phonograph, the stock ticker, and three hundred other devices. What good was electric light in a city already lit by gas?

Edison was famous, but he was not rich — yet. Lighting even a small section of New York would cost a fortune. To get funding from bankers, who knew little about electricity, he would have to prove that electric lighting could be cheaper than gas. Edison made a study of New York's financial district. He calculated the gas cost per lamp, then invited financiers to his laboratory in Menlo Park, New Jersey. There, five hundred bulbs burned more brightly and steadily than gas lamps, and, as Edison proved with his calculations, they could be sold to thousands of customers.

As much businessman as inventor, Edison had formed several companies to promote his other inventions. Although the mayor and the gas companies fought him, several bankers and the city's board of aldermen backed the Edison Illuminating Company's scheme for a power plant near Wall Street. With city approval, Edison bought an empty brick building at 257 Pearl Street in lower Manhattan. After removing walls, his workers installed iron girders and beams and, on the ground floor, installed a boiler to make steam power for the dynamos upstairs.

But there was still the problem of equipment. The Edison Lamp Company made bulbs, but no factories made fuses, switches, or sockets. Edison had to design these, then work with machine shops to make thousands of each. Because telegraph wires clogged the streets, Edison ran current underground through copper rods encased in steel and insulated by hot asphalt. His workers laid fourteen miles of these tubes.

Working day and night, racing from his power plant to his factories, Edison was consumed by the project. "The Pearl Street station was the biggest and most responsible thing I had ever undertaken," he wrote. "What might happen on turning a big current into the conductors under the streets of New York no one could say."

Most uncertain of all were Edison's workers. To men accustomed to horses and buggies, the twenty-two-ton dynamos were the devil's instruments. The engines shook the whole building, shrieked, and gave off sparks, "as if the gates of infernal regions had suddenly opened," one worker said. Once when a malfunction threw parts across the room, workers fled into the streets. Edison had to coax both his equipment and his workers for two exhausting years.

As the project neared completion, Edison signed up customers with the promise of cheaper light. By August 1882, bulbs were installed in the post office, at the *New York Times,* and in fifty other buildings. Edison promised power by certain dates, but date after date passed without any power. Edison was a perfectionist, and he kept testing and retesting to make certain his first try would bring light.

On the morning of September 4, everything was ready. "I had been up most of the night rehearsing my men and going over every part of the system," Edison recalled. "If I ever did any thinking in my life it was on that day."

Arriving at Pearl Street, Edison removed his coat, rolled up his sleeves, and fired up the dynamos in the grimy shop. After several hours of final checks, he walked to the office on Wall Street. With all the delays, his investors had begun to wonder whether this unkempt inventor was a genius or a fool.

At three o'clock, Edison's assistant threw the main circuit breaker at Pearl Street. There was a hum and a crackle as electricity surged beneath the streets. A half mile away, Edison flicked the switch. Instantly, the office was lit by the dazzling glow of a hundred bulbs. The bankers and financiers shouted and clapped Edison on the back. The intense inventor managed a smile.

Within a year, three hundred power stations brought light to hotels, restaurants, and private homes. Electric light spread from a single office in Menlo Park to illuminate the United States and the world. Edison had made good on his promise: "We will make electric light so cheap that only the rich will be able to burn candles."

'I Shall Find a Way, or Make One'

BY GLENNETTE TILLEY TURNER

Richard Theodore Greener distinguished himself in many ways. He was the first African American graduate of Harvard University, in 1870. He earned a law degree while he was a professor and librarian at the University of South Carolina. When the university excluded African Americans at the end of Reconstruction, Greener went to Howard University and became dean of the law school. One of Greener's proudest accomplishments, however, was raising funds to build the magnificent mausoleum known as "Grant's Tomb."

When Ulysses S. Grant ran into financial trouble while living in New York City, local friends came to the rescue. In gratitude, Grant and his wife expressed their interest in being buried in New York. Upon Grant's death in 1885, the mayor of New York wired Mrs. Grant, extending an invitation to bury her husband there. She accepted.

Greener had been a senior at Phillips Academy in Andover, Massachusetts, when the Civil War ended. He and his classmates had idolized General Grant. They had adopted a motto, "I shall find a way, or make one," from the example Grant had set. When Greener was appointed secretary of the Grant Monument Association, he regarded it as a great personal honor. He believed that "like Washington and Lincoln, Grant was risen up by God to lead the Nation in a time of need."

The monument was to be built with private donations. Greener was instrumental in involving individuals and organizations all over New York City. Donation boxes were placed in

Ulysses S. Grant's famous words, "Let us have peace," are carved over the entrance to the General Grant National Memorial.

elevated train stations, and riders contributed nickels and pennies. Churches and community groups encouraged their members to participate. African Americans were especially responsive because of Grant's role in bringing an end to slavery. Philanthropists Cornelius Vanderbilt and J.P. Morgan were on the executive committee of the Grant Monument Association. Greener and General Horace Porter, a member of Grant's staff during the war, gave speeches to help raise money.

After the association raised more than six hundred thousand dollars, an imposing white granite structure in Riverside Park was built high above the Hudson River. Both General and Mrs. Grant are buried there. A display at the memorial tells of Greener's role in making it possible.

Since 1959, the memorial has been operated by the National Park Service. By 1994, the condition of the building and grounds had deteriorated. Grant's descendants considered moving the Grants' bodies to Galena, Illinois, where the Grants had lived before the Civil War. The exterior of the building has since been cleaned up, and the interior has been renovated.

The 135th Street Library

BY GLORIA A. HARRIS

> The library was a center of cultural activity in the 1920s.

The 135th Street Branch of the New York Public Library buzzed with a busy schedule of poetry and book readings, plays, and art shows created by African Americans. In its basement, artists and writers shared their works in progress. Two theater groups met there, and Jessie Fauset, a widely known black woman writer, organized contests, prizes, and exhibitions to encourage Harlem writers and artists. The library was a center of cultural activity in the 1920s.

In the reading room upstairs on the first floor, many famous artists and writers used the Schomburg Collection — books and African objects collected by Arthur Schomburg, a black immigrant from the Caribbean. Schomburg had sold to this library his many books about the life and history of people of African descent. His books were combined with a collection organized the year before at the library and made available to anyone interested in the history and culture of African Americans. Today those books are part of the Schomburg Center for Research in Black Culture.

In 1936, librarian Jean Blackwell Hutson received a telegram to report to the 135th Street Library to work in the Schomburg Collection. Hutson was excited to be working with the famous Mr. Schomburg, and today she recalls much of the activity that made the library a center of the

Harlem Renaissance.

Hutson remembers poets Countee Cullen and Langston Hughes from those days. Cullen, who loved young people and wanted them to know and love literature, earned his living as a teacher. He wrote two books of poems for children in addition to his many books for adults. *The Lost Zoo,* written for children, is a collection of amusing poems about imaginary animals.

Hutson recalls many occasions when she looked up from her desk at the sound of young voices in the doorway. There would be Countee Cullen and his class ready for a visit. He taught French and English at Frederick Douglass Junior High School, located just five blocks from the library. The books in the 135th Street Library had inspired Cullen to write poetry, and he wanted to share these gifts with his students.

Cullen knew the library well. When he was eleven years old, he lived in the Salem Methodist Church parsonage just six blocks away. Even at that young age, he was an excellent poet. As a student, he won poetry prizes at Frederick Douglass Junior High School. In 1925, when he was only twenty-two years old, his first book of poems, *Color,* was published.

The 135th Street Library was one of the first places Langston Hughes visited when he arrived in Harlem in 1921. Whenever Hughes came to the library, Hutson remembers, he wanted to talk with everyone around him. His good humor was contagious, and young people loved to listen to him.

Both Cullen and Hughes, like many other writers and artists of the Harlem Renaissance, wanted to express their feelings about the discrimination and prejudice suffered by African Americans. Cullen expressed his outrage in well-crafted lyrical poems. Hughes used humor and jazz rhythms to voice his protest against the mistreatment of his people. Despite their differences in style, they and others came to the 135th Street Library to learn about their history, create their own contributions to literature, and share their creations with each other.

The library continues to be a source of inspiration for the writers and artists of Harlem and the world. And it still provides people with an opportunity to pursue literary and artistic work.

The Flatiron Building

BY JAMES CROSS GIBLIN

New York is a city famous for its buildings. Perhaps no building is more famous than the Flatiron Building. For more than ninety years, artists have painted it, photographers have taken pictures of it, and visitors to New York City have looked up at it in awe.

It did not always have such an odd name. When it was erected in 1902, it was called the Fuller Building. But it soon acquired the nickname by which it has been known ever since. The building extends from Twenty-second to Twenty-third Street in Manhattan, where Fifth Avenue and Broadway cross each other as they head north and form a triangle. Its triangular shape resembles that of a flatiron (an iron that was heated on a stove rather than working on electricity). People used flatirons to press their clothes at the turn of the century.

Although its narrow, triangular form makes it seem quite tall, the Flatiron Building has only twenty stories. Yet when it was new, it was one of the tallest buildings in New York City — and one of the first to be called a skyscraper.

A building that scrapes the sky is a poetic way of describing a building of great height constructed on a steel skeleton. When the first electric elevator was installed in 1889, the way was opened for the development of the skyscraper. Until then, few buildings were more than six or seven stories tall, since people could not comfortably climb stairs that went higher than that. But new construction methods had to be perfected before the dream of

The Flatiron Building is no longer one of the tallest buildings in New York City, but this photograph, taken a few years after it was built in 1902, shows the building looming over its neighbors.

a skyscraper could become a reality.

The earliest tall buildings were of stone masonry construction with thick walls on the lower floors to support the upper ones. The design was followed by one in which an iron frame supported the floors and the masonry walls bore their own weight. Finally, engineers invented a metal frame sturdy enough to support both the floors and the walls.

The first building in which the new metal frame was used went up in Chicago in 1883. Until the end of the nineteenth century, one skyscraper after another was built in Chicago. Then in 1902, the Flatiron Building, constructed on a metal frame, helped to bring the idea of the skyscraper to New York.

Not everyone liked the Flatiron Building. English artist Sir Philip Burne-Jones, who visited New York in 1902, called it "a vast horror." However, American journalist John Corbin admired its dramatic thrust and said it dominated the nearby avenues like "an ocean steamer with all Broadway in tow." The famous British author H.G. Wells expressed the feelings of many people when he wrote in 1906, "I found myself agape, admiring a skyscraper — the prow of the Flatiron Building to be particular, ploughing up through the traffic of Broadway and Fifth Avenue in the late afternoon light."

As far as height goes, the Flatiron Building was soon eclipsed by the 47-story Singer Building (1908) and the 60-story Woolworth Building (1913), both in lower Manhattan. From the 1920s to the present, skyscrapers in New York have gone on to ever-greater heights with the Chrysler Building (1930, 77 stories), the Empire State Building (1931, 102 stories), and the twin towers of the World Trade Center (1973, 110 stories). But the Flatiron Building still "[ploughs] up through the traffic" of the avenues and commands the attention of New Yorkers and visitors alike.

Based on "New York's First Skyscraper," © 1979 by the New York Kid's Catalog, a New York Partnership. Used by permission of the author.

New York's Treasure Chest

BY STAFF AT THE MUSEUM OF
THE CITY OF NEW YORK

The Museum of the City of New York collects, cares for, and exhibits material relating to the history of New York City and its people. The more than 1.5 million objects in the museum's collections were made, worn, or used by New Yorkers over the past three centuries.

In addition to galleries displaying the permanent collections, the museum has many special, changing exhibitions. Only a small portion of the permanent collections are on display at any one time.

The museum's Paintings Collection includes portraits, landscapes, cityscapes, and scenes from daily life. The Prints and Photographs Collection shows how people and sections of the city have looked since the 1880s. The Decorative Arts Collection includes items such as furniture, utensils, and musical instruments. The Period

One of the most popular galleries at the museum is the Fire Gallery. In the center of the gallery are three pieces of firefighting equipment dating from the 1800s. The Americus Six engine dates from 1851. Two rows of men pumped this double-brake engine by hand to create the pressure necessary to force the water out of the tank. From the time Europeans settled in New York to the mid-1860s, fires were fought by unpaid volunteers. Not only did the volunteer firemen operate the fire engines, hose carriages, and ladder trucks, but they also pulled the equipment to the fire. Horses were not used on a regular basis until after steam engines were introduced in the 1850s.

The museum's Toy Collection includes thousands of dolls, toys, games, and dollhouses. The earliest piece dates from the mid-1700s, the most recent from the 1990s. This horse-drawn omnibus dates from about 1860. It is a toy version of the actual omnibuses that traveled along Broadway, Fifth Avenue, and other New York City streets at that time.

Alcoves in the museum are arranged as rooms from different periods in New York's past. Items from the Theater Collection include costumes from Broadway musicals and stage set models from *The Secret Garden.*

Tours are available for all ages. Public programs offered on weekends and during school vacations include family workshops, family performances, special holiday events, walking tours, lectures, and concerts.

More Famous Places

●●

N ew York City has a rich history of famous places. You have visited many of them in this section. Following is a "taste" of some of the other places historically associated with the Big Apple.

By 1840, New York City was the busiest seaport in the nation. The **South Street Seaport Museum,** which was established in 1967, is an eleven-square-block historic area located on the east side of lower Manhattan. Consisting of galleries, historic ships, and restored buildings, the museum preserves the maritime history of New York City during the nineteenth century.

The **American Museum of Natural History** (which dates from 1869) features dinosaur skeletons, models of ancient animals in realistic settings, and a thirty-four-ton meteor that crashed to earth. Special shows at the Hayden Planetarium (located next to the museum) include space voyages and close-up views of other planets in our solar system.

Founded in 1870, the **Metropolitan Museum of Art,** the city's largest museum, contains art from around the world. You can view costumes, paintings, and sculpture from many different periods in history, armor that medieval knights and their horses wore, and an Egyptian temple.

Rockefeller Center was built between 1929 and 1940 by John D. Rockefeller, Jr., one of the country's business leaders and a famous philanthropist (a person who gives generously to charitable causes). Rockefeller also donated the land for the headquarters of the United Nations. Today Rockefeller Center is a giant business and

Rockefeller Center

entertainment complex consisting of nineteen buildings, including Radio City Music Hall, NBC Studios, and the Time-Life Building.

The **United Nations** was founded in 1945, shortly after World War II, to promote world peace. In 1952, it moved into its headquarters near the East River. Visitors can listen to meetings of delegates from all over the world by using headphones that pro-

vide translations into English, French, Spanish, Russian, Chinese, and other languages.

The *Intrepid* **Sea-Air-Space Museum** is an actual World War II aircraft carrier, docked at a pier on the Hudson River. The flight deck, where airplanes once took off and landed, is as long as three football fields.

Alligators in New York's Sewers

BY SIDNEY HORENSTEIN

It was another one of those sweltering summer days in Florida in the 1930s when the Jones family stopped at a roadside stand for some orangeade to make their sightseeing trip a little more pleasant. In a short time, the children came running to their parents, shouting, "We want one!"

What they wanted was a baby alligator. At that time, it seemed that they were for sale everywhere. Baby alligators are striking because they are nearly black with yellow bands running across their bodies and tails. The children thought it would be great fun to take one or two back home to New York as pets.

After much pleading, the parents relented, and the Joneses had a new family member. Enclosed in a large fish tank, the alligator also became useful as a living "garbage pail" for leftovers. As a result, it grew larger and larger and began to outgrow its urban home. The parents could see that at some future date, the alligator would have to be transferred to a much larger tank, perhaps the bathtub. They could not allow this to happen.

Late one evening, the father wrapped the alligator securely and,

> Eventually, the sewers were full of eight-foot alligators, large enough to be people-eaters and a threat to workers cleaning and repairing pipes.

holding it under his arm, carried it to the nearest sewer. Down it went into the dark, smelly hole, apparently gone forever. This scene was repeated many times, as Florida had become a favorite vacation spot, resulting in the transfer of numerous young alligators out of their natural environment northward into city apartments.

The alligators grew even larger in their new urban sewer environment, and the population grew as a result of new additions and the hatching of baby alligators. Eventually, the sewers were full of eight-foot alligators, large enough to be people-eaters and a threat to workers cleaning and repairing pipes. Crews with rifles were sent out to kill the dangerous reptiles. The workers tried to kill all of them, but it is not certain whether they did because there are still occasional reports of alligator sightings.

This story is my favorite natural history myth from New York City, but it is only one of many myths and legends that have originated in this city. I think that the alligator legend got started in 1932 when a group of boys were shoveling newly fallen snow into a manhole next to the Harlem River. At that time, it was not an unusual way to clear off streets and sidewalks. Several boys pitched snow to another boy who stood beside the open manhole. As he was pushing snow into the dark opening, he saw something thrashing below in the murky soup. With a rope obtained from a nearby hardware store, the boys were able to snag the animal and pull it up to the surface.

The alligator was extremely sluggish and not in very good shape. No one knows for certain, but the alligator was believed to have been thrown off a passing vessel and to have swum into the sewer opening from the river.

As with all legends, there is some factual basis to this one. Over the years, many genuine reports of alligators have been traced to the release of unwanted pets or animals discarded by traveling circuses. They have been found in rivers, lakes, and reservoirs, however, not in sewers. Many other reported sightings have been hoaxes, while still others have not been verified at all. Even the report that five alligators have been found in the sewers over the years is suspect. The alligators were reported to measure four or five inches long, but alligators are usually eight inches long when they hatch.

One story revolves around a group

of boys playing along the Bronx River. They claimed that they spotted a group of alligators swimming downriver. They managed to kill one of the alligators and brought the head to the police. Police investigators did not find the rest of the alligator, nor did the large search party find any trace of the group of alligators supposedly swimming in the river.

True or not, this story made the headlines, and a few other alligator incidents having nothing to do with sewers caught reporters' and the public's attention. Reporters asked workers if they had seen any alligators in the sewers, and soon the legend grew. Eventually, the legend inspired books and even a movie. One official in the Environmental Protection Agency stated that the joke around the office went something like this: "We can't verify whether sewers have alligators in them because every time we send out a crew to check, they never come back."

Alligators are not found naturally in New York City partly because they require a warmer environment. In addition, they probably would have a difficult time reaching Manhattan, the source of all sewer legends.

Alligators typically live in fresh water, and the rivers surrounding Manhattan are probably too salty for them. The water around New York also is probably too cold for alligators. Even in Florida, alligators burrow into mud during a cold snap to keep warm. They cannot do that in a sewer. Nor do sewers provide the fish, frogs, and similar prey that alligators eat. All things considered, alligators could not — and do not — survive there.

But legends die harder than alligators. Every time a story about an alligator appears in the newspaper or on television, it reinforces the legend, even though many years separate the individual events. Perhaps it is as one official surmised. Everyone knows about the sewers in Paris and Vienna, but the New York sewers' only claim to fame is the alligators. He hoped that too much investigation would not destroy the alligator legend, saying, "There should be some romance about everything."

HISTORY
FOR THE FUTURE:
MAKING A TIME CAPSULE

* *

*Show people of the future what New York City is like today by creating
a New York time capsule. Time capsules are one way that we can
preserve something of today for historians of the future.*

Often when a new building is erected or a class graduates from high school or college, the people involved place a time capsule in the building's cornerstone or bury it in the ground. In the case of a graduating class, the time capsule is usually dug up at the class's twenty-fifth reunion. But a time capsule in a building may not be uncovered for several generations. When it is, it will give historians of that time some valuable primary source material to help them understand the past.

Anyone can create a time capsule. You may want to do so as a family or neighborhood project or with your class at school. Soil and weather conditions vary greatly around the country,

so we suggest that you ask a science teacher, soil conservationist, or forester about how best to bury the capsule in your area.

For an individual, family, or small group project, your time capsule can be a large glass jar with a wide mouth and screw-on lid (like the jars in which restaurants buy mustard or pickles). For a large school project, ask your custodian for a thirty- or fifty-gallon drum (such as those in which cleaning fluids come). No matter what kind of container you use (metal, glass, or plastic), the most important things to remember are that all items to be put in your capsule must be as dry as possible and your container must be as full as possible to keep out air.

Here is how to prepare and bury your capsule.

1. Collect materials that have particular meaning for you, your family, your town, or your school. Choose items that are current and perhaps unique to this time. Think about what you would like to find if you were to discover the time capsule.

2. Allow all the items, including the container, to dry thoroughly. Place them in a warm, moisture-free place for two to four weeks. While they dry, prepare a stone or metal marker for the burial site.

3. Wrap each dry item separately in plastic, then force out the air. Do this by piling heavy books on flat items (such as photos or newspaper clippings) or by sucking the air out of other packages.

4. Place each item in the container, packing the items so there is as little air as possible between them. Fill any air spaces with Styrofoam packing pieces. Pack as tightly as possible.

5. Seal the container immediately. Put heavy plastic over the mouth of the container and put the lid over that. Trim excess plastic around the rim and seal the lid with paraffin. Let the container sit a day to allow the seal to harden. The lid on a metal container can be welded shut. Putting your container inside a larger one and sealing the space in between provides double protection.

6. Prepare a hole in the ground twelve to eighteen inches deep or below the frost line in areas where the ground freezes in winter. In areas where the soil is very wet, dig a deeper hole and fill the bottom with gravel for good drainage. Bury your capsule on a dry day.

7. Mark the site with a metal or stone marker indicating when the capsule was buried and when it should be dug up.

BOOKS TO READ

Kidding Around New York City: A Young Person's Guide *by Sarah Lovett* (Santa Fe, New Mexico: John Muir Publications, 1993) includes interesting facts about the city in a tour of fun places for children to visit. Grade 4 and up.

The Brooklyn Bridge: The Story of the World's Most Famous Bridge and the Remarkable Family That Built It *by Elizabeth Mann* (New York: Mikaya Press, 1996) tells the story of the Roebling family and their dedication to building what was then the world's longest bridge. Grade 3 and up.

Dear Bronx Zoo *by Joyce Altman and Sue Goldberg* (New York: Avon Books, 1992) answers the questions most frequently asked in kids' letters about the zoo's animals and activities. Grades 3 to 6.

MORE MEDIA

The Fighting I (A&E, 1995). This fifty-minute video traces the history of the USS *Intrepid* through its service in World War II to its transformation into a museum. Contact museum shop: (212) 957-7062.

Treasures of the American Museum of Natural History. This CD-ROM takes you through the museum's exhibitions of fossils, endangered species, dinosaurs, and more. Contact museum: (212) 769-5000, ext. 4741.

River of Steel (Direct Cinema Limited, 1992). New York City could not have grown as it did without its large, complicated system of underground transportation. This half-hour video tells the story of the city's subway. Contact New York City Transit Museum: (718) 243-8601.

PLACES TO VISIT

All of the famous places discussed in this section, including **Central Park, the American Museum of Natural History, South Street Seaport, the Metropolitan Museum of Art, and the *Intrepid* Sea-Air-Space Museum,** are great places to visit with your family. Here are some others.

Empire State Building. It is no longer the tallest building in the world, or even in New York, but this 1931 skyscraper is still a well-known symbol of the city, and you can still see great views from its 102nd floor.

New York City Transit Museum. An old subway station in Brooklyn was converted into a museum with public transportation exhibits, train models, a working signal tower, and eighteen full-size old subway cars.

3

The Golden Door

NEW YORK IS THE LARGEST CITY IN THE UNITED STATES AND ONE of the largest cities in the world. But what makes our city unique is its people. We come from every part of the world — from Africa, Asia, South America, and other parts of North America. New York City has the most diverse, or mixed, population in the world.

Come meet some of the immigrants who left the country of their birth behind to begin a new life in New York. Some arrived long ago. Some just came yesterday. All have contributed to the culture, or way of life, of New York and the United States.

For more than one hundred years, the Statue of Liberty, standing in New York Harbor, has been a symbol of the United States. It has welcomed millions of immigrants to this country. But did you know that "Miss Liberty" was a gift from the people of France? Take a ferry to this magnificent statue and find out the whole story.

Until the 1950s, most immigrants arrived by boat. And most of them had to stop at Ellis Island before entering the United States. At Ellis Island, they were examined by doctors, and some were turned away because they were ill. Today the huge building that millions of immigrants passed through is open to the public. When you visit, if you are very quiet, you can almost hear pieces of the conversations in many languages from long ago.

Life often was very difficult for new immigrants. They had heard that the streets of New York were paved with gold. But many worked long hours, six or seven days a week, just to be able to feed their families. Children as young as six years old worked to help their families. Look at some of the photographs taken by Lewis Hine and Jacob Riis in the late 1800s and early 1900s. They helped bring attention to these problems.

Jews, Irish, Ghanaians, Haitians, Chinese. These are just a few of the immigrants you will meet. You will visit some of the many neighborhoods of our city, hear many languages, and eat many kinds of food.

When you are through, you will have a chance to prepare your own New York menu.

American Immigrants

In recent years, Indians are sometimes given the name "Native Americans." This is because we know the people Columbus named Indians were the first people to live on the North American continent. But strictly speaking, the very first Native Americans were not natives of North America. They were immigrants.

Sound confusing? If we take a moment to define a few words, the picture becomes clearer.

The word *native* has to do with where a person was born or where something got its start. If you were born in Canada, you are a native of Canada. Even if you later become a citizen of another country, you are still a native of Canada. To move from your native land to another place is to *emigrate*. If your family moved from Canada to the United States, we would say that you emigrated from Canada. Once you settled in the United States, you would be considered *immigrants.* An easy way to keep these terms straight is to remember that you *emigrate* from one place and you *immigrate* to another.

The first Indians in North America were natives of Asia. Many scientists believe that they immigrated to North America by crossing a land bridge thousands of years ago. These Indians were North America's first immigrants.

Why do people emigrate? There are many reasons, but usually they have something to do with a desire for greater freedom or for a better life. When times are hard in a region or a

The great variety found within our nation and culture should serve as a constant reminder to us that the United States is indeed a nation of immigrants.

nation, the people living there are often forced to go elsewhere if they are to survive. War, poverty, and famine are some of the drastic situations that cause large numbers of people to emigrate. In addition, some people have left their native lands through the years because emigrating gave them a sense of adventure or for other personal reasons.

During the 1800s, a period when millions of immigrants came to this country, the United States was considered a land of fabulous opportunity. These were the United States' growing years. There was an abundance of new jobs and open land. People who lived ordinary lives or lives of poverty in other nations felt life would be better for them in the United States. Some had been told that the streets in America were paved with gold and that everyone who lived in this country became rich.

Immigrants who believed these stories were disappointed when they arrived on these shores. What they often found in the United States was hard work and low pay. Those without relatives in this country to welcome them frequently felt out of place because of their foreign language and culture. Some were even met with unfair laws that denied them the rights enjoyed by others in the United States. Still, many immigrants did indeed manage to build better lives for themselves in the United States, and a few did become wealthy and successful in this "promised land."

"Melting pot" is another term that has been used to describe the United States. America and its culture were formed by a unique combination of people from many other nations and their cultures. We might view each segment of our population as an ingredient in the pot. But despite the "melting" that has taken place over the years, different groups of immigrants have never completely lost their individual identities. The substance found in the melting pot is more like a chunky stew than a smooth soup!

The great variety found within our nation and culture should serve as a constant reminder to us that the United States is indeed a nation of immigrants.

'A Gift of the Whole People'

BY KATHLEEN KEENAN

ne Hundred Thousand Dollars!" *The World,* a New York newspaper, printed this victorious headline on August 11, 1885. Patriotic Americans of all ages had contributed enough pennies, nickels, and dimes to help a dream come true. The Statue of Liberty would have a pedestal, a base on which to stand.

The Statue of Liberty was designed by a young French sculptor named Frédéric Auguste Bartholdi. A friend of Bartholdi's suggested the idea of a monument to "liberty, equality, and fraternity" (the motto of the French Revolution) built by French and American craftsmen. Liberty Enlightening the World would represent the friendship between the two countries.

Bartholdi traveled to the United States eager to explain the project to officials. He arrived in 1871, wide-eyed at the vast size of the country. If everything in America was so big, the people would surely appreciate his 151-foot statue! The men Bartholdi met, including President Ulysses S. Grant, were polite but wanted to see the work in progress before giving approval.

Back in Paris, Bartholdi rented a spacious studio. The air filled with the rhythm of mallets pounding sheets of copper as talented craftsmen labored to complete the project.

Money was scarce. In Paris, the Franco-American Union, which managed the Statue of Liberty project, planned fundraising activities. Dinners and musicals featured liberty themes. Miniature copies of the statue, engraved with the buyer's name, were sold. Despite his hectic schedule,

Since 1886, the Statue of Liberty has stood at the entrance to New York Harbor.

Bartholdi made many speeches, and audiences contributed generously.

The French expected such an important project to be a combined effort, with Americans supplying the pedestal for the statue. But few U.S. funds were donated. Many Americans mistakenly believed that the statue was a gift only to New York, since Bartholdi had chosen Bedloe's Island in New York Harbor as the site for his statue. Millionaires preferred to spend their money on luxuries. The Statue of Liberty was ready to be shipped. Would the pedestal be ready in time?

This lack of interest angered Joseph Pulitzer, owner of *The World*. A Hungarian immigrant, Pulitzer strongly believed in the freedom symbolized by the statue. His editorial of March 16, 1885, changed America's mind.

Pulitzer wrote that the Statue of Liberty was "a gift of the whole people of France to the whole people of America." He challenged his readers to give as the French had done and promised to print the name of every donor, regardless of the amount offered. The response was incredible.

Soon the daily list of contributors occupied a full page in *The World*.

Pulitzer also published letters he received, especially from the poor, the elderly, and schoolchildren. Some students wrote of class projects in which they collected money. Although most people could give less than a dollar, through determination and sacrifice, one hundred twenty thousand Americans raised one hundred thousand dollars in only five months.

Work on the pedestal could now resume. Into the mortar of the last stone, a workman tossed a handful of coins as a "thank-you" to all who had made it possible.

The dedication date was set for October 28, 1886. Because of heavy fog, even Bartholdi was unable to view his masterpiece ahead of time. He counted the minutes until he would have the honor of introducing "Miss Liberty" to her people.

Bartholdi tugged at a cord, releasing the red, white, and blue French flag that had covered the statue's face. Thousands of onlookers clapped, cheered, and shouted. Together, the United States and France had created an inspiring monument for people everywhere and a reminder of their love of democracy and abiding friendship.

Gateway to America

BY SHARI LYN ZUBER

As the steamship navigated up New York Bay, sixteen-year-old William Cline stood at the ship's rail, watching the most beautiful sight of the New World pass into view. This stern-looking guardian of New York Harbor was known as Lady Liberty, Liberty Enlightening the World, and the Statue of Liberty. But to this young Hungarian immigrant in 1902, a hint of kindness in the face of the copper-clad statue reminded him of the mother he had lost in Europe. To him, the uplifted torch in one hand and the book engraved with July 4, 1776, in the other symbolized the lighting of a path to a new life and the hope of an independence he had not known in his homeland.

The ship continued northward, as William and the other passengers nervously awaited their arrival at Ellis Island, called both the Island of Hope and the Island of Tears. All on board were dressed in their best clothes to impress the officials and prove that they were worthy of becoming Americans.

Ellis Island, located between Jersey City, New Jersey, and lower Manhattan, first opened its doors as a Federal Immigration Station on January 1, 1892. It replaced Castle Garden in lower Manhattan, which had been used for this purpose from 1855 to 1890. Five years after Ellis Island

The main building on Ellis Island was the first stop for millions of immigrants to the United States.

opened, a fire destroyed the immigration center, which remained closed until December 17, 1900.

When William's ship finally landed at a pier in lower Manhattan, the passengers who had traveled first and second class were allowed to disembark. The others, including William, had to wait for the U.S. Immigration Service ferry to take them across the harbor to Ellis Island. From the ferry, the passengers could see a gigantic red and white building that looked like a palace. In this building, the authorities would decide whether the immigrants could stay in America or must return home.

Once on the island, the immigrants stood beneath a canopy that extended from the main building to the dock's edge. The doors of the building suddenly opened, and some officials emerged to usher in the waiting crowd. The great test was about to begin.

William followed the others to the baggage room, where they deposited their belongings. As they climbed the stairs to the registry room, inspectors watched for obvious medical problems. Those who appeared to have problems would have to undergo thorough medical exams.

William was directed to a winding maze of pipe railings on the second-floor balcony, where doctors checked his general health. Then he was sent to the registry room, also known as the Great Hall. There people stood in long lines, waiting for interpreters to translate the inspectors' questions.

William told the inspector who questioned him why he had come to America and that he would be living with his uncle, who had a job for him. The inspector was satisfied with William's answers and passed him through. William went to the money exchange to change his Hungarian coins for American dollars and boarded the ferry back to Manhattan, where his uncle lived.

Ellis Island and the Statue of Liberty have gone through many changes since William came to America. The statue, France's gift to the United States, was shipped from Europe in pieces and reassembled on Bedloe's Island (now Liberty Island) in 1886. The pedestal on which she stands was built in the United States, paid for largely with pennies donated by schoolchildren.

The statue became a national monument in 1924. The American

Museum of Immigration was established there in 1972 to preserve the heritage of those seeking freedom on these shores. Today an exhibit tells the history of the statue. Visitors climb the spiral staircase to the statue's crown and to enjoy a breathtaking view of neighboring islands and surrounding states.

Ellis Island, originally encompassing three acres, was gradually enlarged to 27.5 acres by adding landfill as the number of immigrants increased. The complex eventually included three connected islands with hospitals, dormitories for those who remained on the island overnight, a bakery, and a rooftop playground for children.

During World War I, immigration decreased, and the island was used to house prisoners of war. As immigration laws became stricter in the 1920s, fewer people passed through Ellis Island, and it became a holding center for those being deported. During World War II, the Coast Guard used it as a training center. The center closed in 1954, but President Lyndon Johnson made it part of the Statue of Liberty National Monument in 1965. It opened for limited tours in 1976 but closed again in 1984 for repairs.

In 1982, the Statue of Liberty–Ellis Island Foundation was established to raise funds for the restoration and preservation of the statue and Ellis Island. On July 4, 1986, a centennial celebration was held in honor of the renovated Statue of Liberty. Four years later, on September 10, 1990, Ellis Island, restored to the way it looked between 1918 and 1924, reopened as an immigration museum.

About half of all Americans can trace their roots to an ancestor who passed through Ellis Island. Both it and the Statue of Liberty pay tribute to the approximately twelve million immigrants who, like William, left their homeland to find a better life in the United States. William's story is part of America's story. It is also the story of my grandfather.

Lewis Hine and the Children of Ellis Island

BY MARY LOU BURKET

At first Lewis Hine saw only the children — a boy with a sack on his back and his little sister, her finger at her lip. They stood holding hands before the huge pile of luggage. But where was their own luggage, brought with them in the steamship across the Atlantic?

As the crowds parted, Hine saw the mother, holding her fretful baby. Her expression was difficult to describe. It was mostly one of worry, caution, and tired fright.

Hine approached the family. He spoke quietly in English, though he knew they could not understand the words. Smiling, he fumbled with his tripod, set his bulky camera upon it, and prepared the large glass plate he would use to take their picture. All the while, he talked and gestured to keep them where they huddled or to move them an inch or two one way or another. They had probably never faced a camera before.

Quickly, Hine looked through the lens, lit the flash, and shot the picture.

This photograph of an Italian immigrant family is one of the many famous images of Ellis Island immigrants to come from the camera of Lewis Hine.

Before the family's eyes had recovered from the flash, Hine left them.

Who was this photographer Lewis Hine? To the more than one million immigrants arriving at Ellis Island during 1905, he was only one more person they had never met and would never meet again. He was a slightly built man with a soft face, whose eyes gleamed behind his delicate glasses. But among the thousands of immigrants, the uniformed officials, the priests, the onlookers, the greeters, the medics, the reporters, and the rest at Ellis Island, Hine did not seem special.

Yet we remember him today. When we think of immigrants arriving on our eastern shore, we often think of them as Lewis Hine saw them.

Hine took pictures at Ellis Island from 1904 to 1909, some of the busiest years for that immigration station. Hine knew the immigrants he saw would change America — and that America would change them. Most were peasants who came from European villages far from the noise of steel mills or the darkness of coal mines. But now they would learn to work in the mills, factories, and mines of the United States. Now they would crowd into the cities and begin new lives.

Their future would be hard, Hine knew. Many of their hopes would not be fulfilled. But Hine admired their dreams and their efforts to make those dreams come true.

In his photos, Hine recorded the hope and fear he saw expressed by many immigrants. He cared especially about the children, thousands of whom would have to work to help support their families.

Between 1908 and 1918, Hine displayed his photos across the country for the National Child Labor Committee, a group of people who hoped to pass laws that would end child labor. Hine photographed children where they worked, though such a thing had rarely been done before. Some called these photographs "stolen." Today we would call them "candid."

In southern textile mills, Hine found girls standing before mighty machines for ten hours each day. Along the Gulf Coast, he found young children working beside their mothers in the seafood canneries, using knives to pick shrimp and crack oyster shells. In Pennsylvania, the photographer saw boys hunched over moving chutes of coal, sorting shale while breathing the dust-filled air. In New York, Hine followed girls and boys into the tenement "sweatshops" where they sat all day, six days a week, sewing in the airless rooms.

Wherever Hine went, he found children — often immigrant children — doing adult work.

A great many people wanted children to work, and to them Hine was the enemy. Factory owners refused to let him past their doors. Foremen threw him out. Parents lied to him.

But Hine was crafty. Acting as a fire inspector, he entered the factories in disguise, measuring the children against his buttons to determine their ages and taking quick notes writing on a pad in his pocket. With notes and pictures as evidence, Hine believed he could persuade Americans to vote to have child labor stopped.

No one else observed the children as Hine did, watching them drag their bare feet through the factory gate in the morning and seeing them dash out at dusk. Because of his photos, and the feelings they provoked in people who saw them, laws were finally passed that took children out of the factories, mines, and sweatshops. The new laws helped to see that children spent their time in schools and on playgrounds.

Hine was a quiet, shy man. Though he took some twenty thousand photographs, many of them as beautiful as fine paintings, he never received much attention for his work, and he never earned much money. When Lewis Hine died in 1940 at the age of sixty-six, he was too poor to pay his rent, and he was discouraged. Too few changes had taken place. Too few eyes had seen his pictures.

Today countless people have viewed and admired Hine's work. His photographs remind us of our immigrant heritage, and they help us to appreciate the difficulty our immigrant ancestors had to overcome.

Crusader
With a Camera

BY TEDD LEVY

Jacob Riis was one of the few outsiders who came to Mulberry Street. The others were usually policemen or undertakers. The heart of Mulberry Street, known as "The Bend," was the center of New York City's slums in the 1880s. It was not the kind of place people visited, but hundreds lived there. Many of the residents of Mulberry Street were immigrants, as Jacob Riis himself had been.

As a boy in Denmark, Riis had been apprenticed to a carpenter in Copenhagen. Unable to find a job as a carpenter, and unable to marry the girl he loved because her father objected, he sailed for America in 1870, when he was twenty-one years old.

Times were hard in America then. And the victims of these difficult times were often the jobless, hungry, and homeless immigrants. Jacob Riis arrived without much money, without a place to live, and with no job. He did chores for meals. He slept in barns and alleys. He once walked from New York to Philadelphia in hopes of finding work with a Danish family he knew there. During the next three years, Riis found employment in Philadelphia as a carpenter, farm hand, lumberjack, laborer, railroad worker, and salesman.

Finally, Riis managed to find a job as a newspaper reporter. He worked hard at this and earned a reputation as a good reporter. With the money he earned, Riis traveled to Denmark for the girl he loved. They were married

and returned to New York City.

Long before Riis and his wife returned to New York, many large, comfortable houses had dotted the countryside in the vicinity of Mulberry Street. Seeing an opportunity to make money, the owners of the old houses began renting rooms. Later, as more people came, the landlords divided the large rooms into smaller ones. Many of these rooms had no windows, so the air became very stale. Soon every available space, from the clammy cellar to the stuffy attic, was divided and rented. These once lovely houses had become tenement buildings and the homes of many immigrants.

The tenements were usually four to six stories high. There was often a store on the first floor. On each of the floors above there lived at least four families. An apartment had one or two dark closet-size spaces, which were used as bedrooms, and a tiny living room. Only partitions separated families, or groups of people, from each other.

An energetic police reporter, Riis covered the life and crimes on Mulberry Street and knew the poor people who lived there in the tenements. By himself or with a policeman, he often went through the slum district between two and four o'clock in the morning, to "see it off its guard," he said. What he saw were people sleeping in alleys and in the filthy, crowded buildings. He saw lodging houses that rented space on their dirty floors to thieves, beggars, and drunks. By day, he saw many homeless children living in the streets begging or stealing food from pushcarts.

The people of Mulberry Street spent most of their time outside. They stayed inside only when they were sick or sleeping. Inside the tenements, the heat was nearly unbearable and there was no fresh air. Heaps of straw and rags served as beds. Broken stoves leaked smoke at every turn of their stacks, and there was no place to throw out rubbish. The smell alone drove people to the street.

"The sight I saw there," Riis said of the slums, "gripped my heart until I felt that I must tell of them or burst. One half of the world does not know how the other half lives," he said. Riis believed the world did not care about its poor, and he set about to change that. He wanted people to care.

Several years earlier, in 1873, the New York Daily Graphic had published the first photograph in a newspaper.

By 1888, a flash had been developed that allowed photographs to be taken in dark areas. It was noisy and clumsy. But it meant that photographs could be taken to show life in the tenements. Riis bought a camera and taught himself how to take pictures.

His photos and newspaper stories brought slum life to everyone's attention. Working late at night, often after giving illustrated lectures, he wrote about the slums. In 1890, he published How the Other Half Lives, a book of writings and photographs portraying life in the slums. It was the first time that the terrible conditions were revealed in photographs. His book was a success.

In 1901, Riis left his job as a newspaper reporter. He worked on several books, including The Battle With the Slum, which told of inadequate schools and playgrounds. His writings and photographs helped to improve the health and safety conditions in tenements.

Jacob Riis waged a lifelong battle to eliminate slums and to improve life for the poor. President Theodore Roosevelt, who was a friend of Riis, once called him "the best American I ever knew."

Street Arabs

BY HEATHER MITCHELL AMEY

Editor's Note: The camera of Jacob Riis revealed many shocking problems of tenement life. Another type of problem that particularly concerned Riis was the existence of thousands of homeless children who lived as vagabonds in the streets. Immigrant and native children alike, they were known as "street arabs."

They could be found on every street corner of New York City in the early years of this century. Many were newsboys, selling their papers with cries of "Extra! Get your extra 'dition!" Others were bootblacks, armed with shoeshine kits and strong sales pitches. A few gambled for a living, and some could pick a pocket as deftly as the Artful Dodger himself.

They were street arabs — boys who fended for themselves and claimed no place as home. A warm steam vent in winter, an abandoned shed, a sheltered spot under a bridge, or even a barrel in an alley were used as shelter by these young boys.

With names like The Snitcher, Slobbery Jack, and The King of Bums,

street arabs were known for their spunky good humor and their generosity toward fellow street rats who were down on their luck. They often ignored the law, but they strictly obeyed their own special code of fair play and swift justice. They were tough, independent, and clever. But they were also very poor and uneducated, and because of this they stood little chance of rising up from their way of life.

To combat this army of vagabonds, a group of citizens established the Children's Aid Society. The purpose of the society was to help the street boys to help themselves. Newsboys' Lodging Houses cropped up here and there across the city — "hotels" for homeless boys. One of the few rules of

"Street arabs" were homeless boys who spent the night wherever they could.

the lodging houses was posted on a sign outside the door: "Boys who swear or chew tobacco cannot sleep here."

If a boy lacked the eighteen cents for his room and board, he was given credit. If he wished to go into honest business selling newspapers or shining shoes, the society loaned him money to get started. Evening classes were held so that street arabs could learn to read and write, giving them a fair chance at steady jobs when they grew older.

Street arabs were proud of their independence, and they felt they did not need or want anyone's charity. The Children's Aid Society did not give charity. Rather, it offered a fair deal, and the street arabs respected and appreciated this. Thanks to the society, and to concerned individuals such as Jacob Riis (see pages 78–80), many of the wandering, homeless street arabs were able to become honest, hard-working, independent citizens.

Through the Golden Door

BY CRAIG E. BLOHM

As the ocean liner SS *Pennland* steamed slowly into New York harbor, throngs of people pushed toward the ship's railings. After a long voyage spent mostly in the cramped spaces below deck, the passengers strained to see the symbol of their new home. Suddenly, out of the mist, appeared the upraised arm and gleaming torch of the Statue of Liberty, welcoming the newcomers to America's "golden door." Cries of joy filled the air. But tears also were shed for a life or family left behind and an uncertain future ahead.

The late nineteenth century saw

The America to which the Jewish immigrants came was far different from their European homeland.

the greatest immigration of Jewish people in history. Between 1880 and 1920, two and a half million Jews from eastern Europe came to America on ships like the *Pennland*. Life in western Russia had seemed promising under Czar Alexander II, who eased many of the restrictions on the Jews. But that ended suddenly when Alexander was assassinated in 1881. Strict anti-Jewish laws returned, and thousands of Jews were killed in pogroms, or government-sponsored massacres. This discrimination, combined with dire poverty, led the eastern European Jews to seek a better life elsewhere. For many, the United States seemed to be the *goldeneh medina* (golden land) for which they longed.

The America to which the Jewish immigrants came was far different from their European homeland. In fact, one writer called it a leap from the "medieval age into [the] 20th century." The newcomers settled in large cities, especially New York. Back in Russia, they had heard that, in America, you could find gold on the city streets. Reality, however, turned out to be quite different.

Most of the Jewish immigrants who stayed in New York lived on the Lower East Side, an area where Irish and Italian immigrants had once lived. In all, about half a million Jews jammed into an area about one and a half miles square. Their homes were crowded tenements, or apartment buildings, with fire escapes in front and cramped living spaces inside. Often several families lived together in one tiny apartment. Below the rundown tenements, the streets swarmed with peddlers hawking their wares, people milling around pushcarts, and children playing noisily in the filthy streets.

"Children owned the streets," wrote Sophie Ruskay, who grew up on the Lower East Side. "There were a few parks, but too distant to be of any use, so the street was the common playground." Boys played baseball or shot marbles, and girls played potsy, a kind of hopscotch.

Having few practical skills, many Jewish immigrants turned to peddling to make a living. With a rented pushcart or going door to door, peddlers could earn a few pennies a day. Others found jobs in the garment industry, which had been started by German Jewish immigrants decades earlier. Working in overcrowded sweatshops, men, women, and children toiled twelve to seventeen hours a day sewing, ironing, and running heavy machinery. Newspaperman Jacob Riis (see pages 78–80) reported hearing "the whir of...sewing machines, worked at high pressure from earliest dawn till mind and muscle give out together."

Despite such terrible working conditions, the Jewish immigrants could take refuge in their community. In the Old World, they had the shtetls, small towns where most of the population was Jewish. After crossing the ocean, Jewish people tried to continue the closeness of these towns, They formed *landsman-shaftn,* social organizations of Jews from the same shtetl. These societies helped immigrants by providing them with medical insurance, loans, and other aid. Settlement houses offered social services and were places of education and recreation.

Religion also kept the new Jewish immigrants together. The Jews placed great importance on their faith. But the Orthodox, or traditional, Judaism of the eastern European immigrants often clashed with the more liberal Reform Judaism of the German Jews. And it was sometimes difficult to maintain a religion-centered life with all the demands of making a home in a strange land. The synagogue helped these immigrants keep in touch with an important part of their heritage.

Until immigration was restricted in the 1920s, thousands of Jewish immigrants gazed with hope upon the Statue of Liberty. "Send these, the homeless, tempest-tost to me," reads the plaque at the base of the statue. "I lift my lamp beside the golden door!" How fitting that Emma Lazarus, the author of these welcoming words, was herself an American Jew.

Buon Giorno, America!

BY SHARI LYN ZUBER

The railroad platform was alive with the waving, crying figures of relatives bidding farewell to family members as they boarded the train that would take them to the nearest seaport. There, a steamship awaited the hopeful *contadini* (peasants), who planned to find their fortunes on the gold-lined streets of America. The two-week voyage in cramped, filthy steerage seemed a small price to pay for liberating one's family from the squalor and dead-end life of Italy's Mezzogiorno, "the land that time forgot."

The Italian people had endured hundreds of years of domination by foreign monarchs and exploitation by feudal lords. By 1848, Giuseppe Mazzini and Conte Camillo Benso di Cavour were leading a movement called the Risorgimento, which demanded a constitutional government and the unification of Italy. From 1859 to 1870, Giuseppe Garibaldi, with the aid of France and Prussia, relentlessly fought to free Italy from Austrian domination.

The reunification of Italy under one government in 1870 failed to close the gap between northern and southern Italians that had developed over the centuries. The north had long been the nation's cultural center, had the best farmland, and had the best facilities for modernizing and industrializing the newly unified country.

In the south, wealthy absentee landlords charged peasants high rents, demanding the majority of the tenant farmers' harvests in exchange for using the land. In the late nineteenth and early twentieth centuries, volcanic eruptions and earthquakes destroyed more than three hundred southern villages, and bacterial diseases decimated the vineyards.

News of life in America trickled back to the contadini from relatives and friends who had emigrated to the United States. The glowing reports of freedom and the opportunity to grow rich encouraged the southerners to hazard the voyage to the New World.

Prior to 1850, most of the five thousand Italians who had settled in the United States were well-educated northerners. Between 1880 and 1914, however, of the nearly four million Italians who arrived in America, eighty percent came from the Mezzogiorno (the region south of Rome) and from Sicily.

More than three-quarters of the immigrants were men who had made the difficult decision to leave their families behind in Italy. They hoped to become wealthy in America and return to Italy so that the entire family could live in comfort in their homeland. Indeed, more than one-third of all Italian immigrants

eventually returned to Italy. Some were successful, others disillusioned. Many of the immigrants who stayed in the United States saved their meager earnings and sent money for their families to join them here.

Although most immigrants were eager to work, finding a job was difficult. Before 1885, *padroni* (labor contractors) recruited peasants in Italy for work in the United States. In an effort to protect immigrants from unscrupulous labor contractors, Congress outlawed this practice in 1885. In response, the padroni merely shifted their base of operations to America. In exchange for providing temporary food and lodging and finding employment for immigrants, the padroni took a hefty percentage of the newcomers' salaries. Unable to speak English, and generally illiterate in Italian, too, the contadini had no choice but to accept the padroni's terms.

As more Italians came to America, social and religious organizations, such as the Society for the Protection of Italian Immigrants, were founded to spare them the injustices of the padrone system. The societies would find housing and jobs for immigrants and provide legal and medical aid.

Many of the immigrants settled

near their port of entry, which was either Ellis Island in New York City or elsewhere along the eastern seaboard. Searching for people who came from their village or region, the newcomers congregated in urban communities called "Little Italies." The living conditions in these overcrowded neighborhoods were terrible, but there was hope that things would get better. The neighborhoods provided a sense of familiarity that lessened the newcomers' homesickness and loneliness. East Harlem and Mulberry Street Bend in New York City, Federal Hill in Providence, Rhode Island, and Boston's North End were only a few of the famous Italian neighborhoods of the immigration era.

The modernization and industrialization of the United States during the late 1800s and early 1900s required a vast resource of unskilled labor. Italian immigrants met that need. Although they were paid less than both white and black Americans, these hard-working, dedicated individuals laid the railroad tracks that connected the nation, worked the mines and quarries, felled the trees that made room for urban expansion, laid the pipes for water systems, paved the streets, built the sub-

ways that facilitated intracity travel, and raised the skyscrapers that made this nation's cities grow to dizzying heights.

Although the majority of the contadini chose pick-and-shovel jobs, some groups worked cooperatively on small tracts of land called truck farms. One of the most successful farming communities was located in Vineland, New Jersey.

Some Italian immigrants settled in California, which became known as the "Italy of America." Establishing themselves primarily in San Francisco's North Beach section, some found great success in the fishing industry, contributing to the growth of Fisherman's Wharf. Others established vineyards that produced some of the world's best wines.

The passage of restrictive immigration laws during the 1920s was an attempt to stem the flood of southern and eastern European immigrants. Because of these laws, Italian immigration dropped to only several thousand per year. But the Italians who had come to the United States in the previous four decades had already made their mark on their new homeland.

PREVENTIVE MEDICINE

BY LINDA PEAVY AND URSULA SMITH

In the early 1900s, fifteen hundred babies died each week in New York City. Dr. Sara Josephine Baker seemed to be almost alone in refusing to accept this situation as unchangeable. If New York City wanted to save babies, she thought, the health department would have to concentrate on preventing them from falling ill at all.

"Preventive medicine" was a relatively new concept in the early 1900s. City officials, and even parents, wondered how she could ask them to spend taxpayers' money on healthy babies when so many babies and children were sick and dying.

Dr. Baker refused to give up. In early summer of 1908, she persuaded the health department to let her train the city's school nurses in preventive health care. Then she sent them out into one particular area of the city to see if teaching mothers how to keep babies healthy could really save lives.

As her nurses heard of a birth, they immediately sought out and examined the newborn and discussed feeding practices with the mother. The nurses also offered some important advice on hygiene. They encouraged the mothers to bathe their infants frequently, to dress them in cool summer clothes, to see that their rooms were well ventilated, and to take them into a tiny nearby park each afternoon for a bit of fresh air. And that was all. There were no magic medicines, no difficult home treatments, just these simple changes.

By summer's end, Dr. Baker had the statistics she needed to prove that these simple changes could save lives. There were twelve hundred fewer deaths in the areas of the city where the nurses had worked than there had been the previous summer, while all the rest of the city showed as many baby deaths as before. Twelve hundred babies had been saved, and Dr. Baker had proved that preventive health care worked.

Home Away From Home: Haitian Life in New York

BY ELIZABETH MCALISTER
WITH KETHELYNE JEAN-LOUIS

The New York area is home to the largest population of Haitians outside Haiti. The Haitian mother tongue, Creole, is the second foreign language after Spanish spoken by students in New York public schools. During the Duvalier dictatorship (1957–1986), huge numbers of Haitians settled in New York to escape poverty and persecution for expressing their opinions of the government.

Haitian people generally live alongside other Haitians in particular neighborhoods in Brooklyn, Manhattan, and other areas of the city. Sometimes several people in a New York neighborhood know one another from their hometown in Haiti. Haitian neighborhoods usually have several central meeting places where people can get the latest news from Haiti and exchange information. They gather in barbershops, record stores, and restaurants to discuss events. Haitian restaurants in Manhattan are favorite stops for taxi drivers who need a break. They go inside, eat some conch stew and rice with peas, and find out the latest about the Haitian government, where they can rent an apartment, or who is marrying whom.

Which language to speak is something Haitian people have to think about. In Haiti, many people speak two languages, French and Creole. When they get to New York, they have to learn English. Sometimes children learn English faster than their parents. Tensions can rise within a family when the children in a household have to help their parents communicate with landlords, hospitals, and schools. Haitian children sometimes have to take on a lot of responsibility for the rest of the family.

Haitian parents are concerned about their children getting the proper education and the right amount of discipline, so many Haitian children go to Catholic schools. You have to wear a uniform, study hard, and obey the rules. Haitian children are taught to respect their elders and help out when needed. Sometimes they live with grandparents, aunts and uncles, and cousins rather than their parents. The family is central to Haitian life, and everyone is expected to pitch in and contribute.

The strength of the family is important in helping many Haitians migrate to New York. In a common system of migration called chain migration, the family in Haiti saves money and sends one person to the United States. When that person finds a job and gets settled, he or she sends a ticket for another person. Together, they send for others. Often a woman comes first because immigrant women usually can find jobs more easily than immigrant men. Haitian women work very hard, often holding more than one job, to support themselves in New York while also sending money home to Haiti.

Haitians in New York rely on each other for the financial and emotional support they need to deal with the tremendous problems they face when they move to the United States. For example, in Haiti they are the majority, but here they are a racial and ethnic minority. When they arrive, they may experience racial discrimination for the first time in their lives. Many people look to the Catholic or Protestant churches for support. Some churches in New York hold services in Creole or French and provide various social services.

Although the Duvalier dictatorship was overthrown in 1986, conditions in Haiti remain unsettled, and large numbers of Haitians continue to make New York City their home.

Keeping the Traditions Alive

BY BEATRICE BERG

Dr. Yaw Antwi (pronounced "yow on-twee") was born in the little town of Bomeng, Ghana, which has a population of ten thousand Asante people. Now Dr. Antwi and his wife and children live in Queens, a borough of New York City, in a huge apartment project that houses twenty-five thousand people of all races, creeds, and colors.

About two thousand Asantes, many of them children, live in New York. They are scattered throughout the city's five boroughs, with the majority in Brooklyn and the second-largest group in the Bronx.

"Many of the children were born in the United States, and some of them have never even been to Africa," Dr. Antwi says. "Ninety percent of the children speak English. Even though they may understand Twi, which is the Asante language, they cannot speak it."

This troubles Dr. Antwi, who has both a master's and a doctorate degree in higher educational administration from Ohio State University. He and his wife make a point of speaking Twi at home with their eleven-year-old American-born daughter Beverly (whose Asante name is Akosua) and even with one-year-old son Jeffrey (Ofori), who cannot yet speak either language.

For some time, a number of Asantes in New York City had been talking informally about forming a group to help each other and especially to educate the younger generation about the traditional culture and language of their own people. In early 1982, some of them decided to do more than just talk. A group of nine Asantes, including Dr. Antwi, called a meeting in Brooklyn. They decided to form an

The Asanteman Association held a parade in June 1991 in celebration of Asante Day.

organization that would hold monthly meetings conducted in the Twi language, and they sent invitations to all the Asante families in the city.

And so the Asanteman Association of the United States of America was born. Its charter states these purposes: "To promote Asante culture among Asantefuo [*fuo* means "people" in Twi] in the U.S.A.; to support and promote the interests of Asantefuo in the U.S.A.; to seek the welfare and education of Asantefuo in the U.S.A.; to foster friendship and understanding among Asantefuo and others."

The emblems of the organization are the Golden Stool and the proverbial porcupine *(otoko)*. Both are symbols of royalty and power for the Asante. A new chief is elected every year.

"This is not the way it is done at home," Dr. Antwi explains. "There, to be chief, a man has to come from a particular royal line. Here, we decided to do it the democratic way and give every member a chance to run for office."

The first elections of the Asanteman Association were held in July 1982. The inauguration that year was a special occasion because Otumfuo Nana Opoku Ware II, the Asantehene

(king) of the Asantes in Ghana, sent one of his chiefs to represent him at the ceremonies. The word "Asantefuohene" means "chief of the Asante people in New York."

Women have always played an important role in Asante life, so a "queen mother" is also elected every year. Dr. Antwi says, "Long before there was a movement for equal rights for women in the United States, the Asantes had women's liberation. In 1900, Yaa Asantewah led an army of men to fight the British. It took them many months to defeat her. The English still call it Yaa Asantewah's War."

Boys and girls are taught the steps and rhythms of the dances done to the throbbing beat of the *adowa* drums. They are called "talking drums" because everything they play has a meaning or a message and the tones of the drums reproduce the tones and rhythms of speech. One such message, for example, would announce the coming of the king.

In addition to these cultural projects, the association has sent shipments of dental equipment and hospital beds to Kumasi, the historic Asante capital in Ghana.

Growing Up in China and New York

BY ALICE YOUNG

The authors of these memoirs are recent immigrants from China. The boys and girls are sixth-graders who live in New York City and attend Public School 1, where they are learning English to help them adjust to their lives in the United States. Sharing memories of their experiences in China allows the children to hold on to their identity and culture, which seem to slip away from them as they blend into American society.

My Two Slippers

When I came to America, my best friend gave me two slippers. I brought the two slippers here. Every time I see the two slippers, I am reminded of my best friend. She lives in China.

A long time ago, my best friend and I were in the same school. She played with me, and we helped each other. First I didn't want to come here because I had a lot of friends in China. But now in America, I have a lot of friends, too.

Lillian Li

Grandmother and the Buddha

My Buddha is very important to me, because when I came to the USA, my grandmother gave it to me. Every time I look at this Buddha, it reminds me of China.

My grandmother was very loving. When we ate dinner, my grandmother always gave me the best piece to eat. She wouldn't let me eat yesterday's food. When I got sick, she didn't sleep until I got better. My grandmother

Alice Young and her students share songs and stories in their New York City classroom.

loved my mother and father, but she loved me more.

When I came to the USA, she cried and told me to go home and listen to my mother and father. I feel I have to remember her. I don't want to get her mad. I want her to be happy forever. Every time she gets sick, I say to myself, "I would give my life for her to get better." I love my grandmother very much. I want her to be happy always.

Danny Zeng

My Bracelet

I came to America last year. One day my aunt went to China to see her cousin and her sister. I asked her to carry something to my cousin, my grandmother, and my grandfather.

When my aunt came back to America, she brought me many things. She gave me a little red bag. When I opened it, I saw a bracelet. She said that my grandmother and grandfather had given it to me, and she said it was real gold. I told my mother, and I put it on my wrist. This was important to me because it was given by my grandmother and grandfather.

My grandmother and grandfather love me very much, and I love my grandmother and grandfather, too. I wrote a letter to China and thanked my grandfather and grandmother. Every time I see the bracelet, I think of my grandmother and grandfather. I feel that I am in China playing with them. When my mother wouldn't give me money to buy candy, my grandfather would give it to me. Sometimes I would sleep with my grandmother. I was very happy in China.

Jiang Na

The Coat

When I came to America, I brought my coat, which my grandmother gave me as a present. Every time I wear the coat, I think of my grandmother and when I lived in China. One day my grandmother and I went apple picking. It was very cold. My grandmother gave me the coat to keep warm. I will never throw away this present because I can keep it for memories of Grandmother.

Bao Feng Zhou

Photograph

On July 4, 1993, my father came back to China from America. My father brought back many things to wear and eat. My father brought back candy and cookies. We ate the candy and cookies. We were very happy. My father took many pictures of us. But these pictures did not have the whole family. We wanted to take family pictures, so we went on the bus to pick a place to take pictures.

When I came to America, I brought the family pictures. When I look at the pictures, I can see that I was ten years old. I can think I am in China. I am happy and sad when I think about China.

Qiao Bai Zheng

THE WEARING OF THE GREEN

BY SHARI LYN ZUBER

Every year on March 17, the life of Ireland's patron saint, Patrick, is commemorated with parades all over the world.

Patrick is thought to have been born in Roman-ruled ancient Britain around 385. His father, Calpurnius, was a local government official and Christian church deacon.

When he was sixteen, Patrick was captured by Irish raiders and sold into slavery in Ireland. He served as a herder for six years until he had a vision telling him to escape. Reaching Gaul (modern-day France), he spent time there studying religion.

In 432, Patrick returned to Irish shores. With a wooden barn as a church, he set about converting the pagan population to Christianity. Despite opposition from local Druid spiritual leaders, Patrick worked relentlessly until his death in about 461.

Many legends developed about St. Patrick, including his driving of the snakes from Ireland and his use of the three-leaved shamrock to explain the Holy Trinity.* (The shamrock is Ireland's national emblem.) What he did for certain was instill the knowledge of Latin and the learning of the Roman Empire in the Irish.

As early as 1737 in Boston, Irish societies in Colonial America celebrated March 17 as a religious holiday. By the late nineteenth century, St. Patrick's Day parades had become yearly events in cities across the United States. Today the largest celebration is up New York City's Fifth Avenue, where more than two hundred thousand people wear green, the color of the Emerald Isle.

*In Christianity, the union of three divine persons — the Father, Son, and Holy Spirit — in one God.

'City to the World'

BY MEG GREENE

H ome to many different cultures, New York has often been called the "city to the world." Some of the best places to experience New York's ethnic and cultural diversity are its neighborhoods. For instance, in Queens, Astoria is home to a large community of Greek immigrants. Brighton Beach, located in Brooklyn, is known as "Little Odessa by the Sea" because of the large number of Russians who settled there. (Odessa is a major Russian port city located on the Black Sea.) Manhattan neighborhoods such as Little Italy and Chinatown still maintain "old country" traditions. Harlem, the "black capital of the country," boasts a rich African American heritage, while the Lower East Side symbolizes New York's "melting pot," with its Jewish, Polish, Italian, and Irish communities.

Little Italy, located in lower Manhattan, attracted thousands of Italians who came to New York in the second half of the nineteenth century. At the center of Little Italy is Mulberry Street, with its wide array of restaurants, open-air markets, social clubs, and businesses. Every September, Mulberry Street is the site of a grand festival honoring St. Gennaro, the patron saint of Naples.

Mulberry Street parallels Mott Street, the center of New York's **Chinatown.** More than a hundred thousand Chinese Americans live in Chinatown's dozen or so winding blocks, where some old tenement buildings are topped by gilded pagodas and the carved figures of red-and-gold dragons.

Like Little Italy, this neighborhood has many restaurants and open-air markets where shoppers can find vegetables, spices, and fruits native to China. Buddhist temples are another reminder of the neighborhood's cultural history. Every winter, thousands of people flood the streets to celebrate the traditional Chinese New Year with parades and dancing.

The **Lower East Side** was once considered one of the most notorious slums in the city. By the 1880s, this crowded neighborhood, with tenements such as "Brick Bat Mansion" and "Gates of Hell," was home to thousands of Jewish immigrants from Germany, Poland, and Russia, as well as Greeks, Turks, Czechs, Bohemians, and Hungarians.

At one point, the Lower East Side had a population density of seven hundred people per acre. Today the Lower East Side is a vibrant community of many ethnic groups, including East Indians. Many people who visit the neighborhood stop at the Lower East Side Tenement Museum to learn more about immigrant life.

Greenwich Village, in lower Manhattan on the west side, has a different character. Once an Algonquian Indian settlement, the Village, with its hodgepodge street patterns, has attracted several generations of writers, musicians, and artists since the late nineteenth century.

The quiet streets and low rents brought many people to the Village, but others came to escape the confines of traditional American society. Known as "bohemians," these men and women gave the Village a reputation for being unconventional and daring. Today the Village, with its galleries, restaurants, and quaint shops, has become a popular spot among tourists.

Harlem, "America's first black Mecca," is located in uptown Manhattan. Once a neighborhood of Dutch, Irish, and German immigrants, Harlem had become home to thousands of African Americans by the early 1900s.

Harlem also became the center for African American culture and thought. The Harlem Renaissance (see pages 197–205) showcased the talents of a number of writers, artists, musicians, and thinkers. Today East Harlem, or Spanish Harlem, is home to people from Puerto Rico, the Dominican Republic, Haiti, and Jamaica.

Any city's character is shaped by its people. For New York City, that character is as varied as the city is large. Despite the many changes that New York City has undergone and will undergo, its neighborhoods are lasting reminders of its exciting and diverse ethnic history.

The Neighborhood Island

• • • • • • • • • • • • • • • • • •

BY BEATRICE BERG

What would you guess is one of the twelve smallest of the almost two hundred important islands on earth? According to *The World Almanac,* Manhattan, one of the five boroughs of New York City and the island on which I live, falls into that category.

A superb harbor made this island a natural port and trade center from the early days of European settlement. As more and more people flooded in, they pushed uptown from the island's southern tip and, finally, up in the air with Manhattan's famous skyscrapers. Now, although the island extends only two and half miles at its widest and twelve and a half miles at its longest, almost one and a half million people are crammed into its twenty-three square miles.

That sounds as though we are packed in like sardines. It even feels that way sometimes when I am trying to squeeze myself into the subway at rush hour. But living here is not like that at all.

Manhattan is not all glitter and spectacular skyscrapers as seen on picture post cards and TV. Rather, it is a collection of neighborhoods, which are somewhat like small towns. There are no definite boundaries, but when you ride a bus or take a walk, you become aware that you are passing through noticeably different "towns." The faces of the people, the languages they speak, the way they dress, the kinds of stores in which they shop, and probably even the buildings in which they live are quite unlike the ones you see ten or twelve blocks away.

A fascinating mix of people and businesses makes the Lower East Side one of the most lively neighborhoods in New York.

If I walk only two blocks south of my twelve-story apartment building to cross Fourteenth Street, I find myself in the neighborhood called the Lower East Side. Here the streets are lined with old five-story walkups (buildings with no elevators) and teeming with dark-haired, animated people ranging in color from white to coffee to choco-late to black, most of them speaking Spanish with the varied accents of Puerto Rico, the Dominican Republic, Cuba, and almost every country in Central and South America.

Mary Help of Christian Church started in a basement in 1911 to serve poor Italian immigrants. They did not have enough money to build the upper church until 1917. It is not an Italian church anymore, however; it is now mostly Hispanic.

That is the way it has been going for about a century and a half. The Lower East Side has been absorbing wave after wave of poor immigrants — Ukrainians, Poles, Jews from eastern Europe, and others — all coming in search of work and, they hope, better lives. People are like birds of a feather — they flock together. They feel more comfortable among others whose language, customs, history, and religion are like their own. That is how ethnic neighborhoods are born.

Many who prosper move on to "better" neighborhoods and to the suburbs, making way for the next wave of newcomers. But some get so attached to their "town" that they stay on, and every group adds to the flavor of the area.

In my neighborhood, narrow little Korean produce stores seem to have sprouted everywhere, with stands piled high with dazzling arrays of fresh fruits and vegetables extending halfway across the sidewalks. Everybody enjoys the open-air shopping, even in winter.

Jae-Sun Shim and his wife, Sun-Sook, have an unusual story to tell.

Jae-Sun majored in political science at Korean University and was deputy editor of the *Seoul Daily News.* Sun-Sook was an art student at Ihwa Women's University.

Jae-Sun became editor in chief of the *Korea Guardian* in Philadelphia after he came to the United States in 1973. "But you can't make money being a newspaperman," he explained. When he heard from a friend that the elderly Di Bellas, Carmine and John, wanted to sell their store and retire, Jae-Sun decided to buy it.

"Italian food is similar to Korean — both use lots of spices and garlic," he said. He read books about Italian cheeses and sausages, and the Di Bellas stayed behind the counter with the Shims for months to teach them the tricks of the trade.

Many candy stores/newsstands in Manhattan are run by East Indians, one of whom said that most of the East Indians who live in downtown Manhattan are from Bangladesh. Formerly a province of India, it became a separate country in 1971 after a devastating war. He also told me that every one of the many Indian restaurants on a single block on Sixth Street is owned by Bangladeshis. It does not seem possible that so many restaurants could be crowded into one block.

As I walked along, a lovely red brick building caught my eye. Chiseled into its white stone pediment are the words "Dedicated to the Glory of God and the Brotherhood of Man." This is a synagogue, actively functioning in a neighborhood where not many Jewish people now live, although it was once one of the most densely populated Jewish neighborhoods on this island.

The building has a sad history. At the turn of the century, when the residents of the neighborhood were mostly of German descent, it was a Lutheran church. On a June day in 1904, the church chartered an excursion boat called the *General Slocum.* The boat caught fire on the East River, and one thousand picnickers, many of them children, were lost. Most of the grieving survivors moved away, and the church stood empty until 1940, when it was rededicated as a synagogue.

At the 2nd Avenue Kosher Deli, you can still get chicken soup with matzo balls just like Jewish grandmothers make. In the 1980s, the owner put in a new sidewalk in which thirty large five-pointed stars are embedded. Each contains the names of two of the great stars of the Yiddish theater, which was once centered in the neigh-

borhood. There is also a long bench where you can rest your feet and watch people stop to inspect this reminder of the past.

This is also Ukrainian country, where you can buy a bowl of *flacksi,* tripe ("innards") soup. The eighty-year-old St. George's Church still flourishes.

Things are changing, however, and not always for the better. A little dry-goods store closes because the landlord demands triple the rent. A real estate speculator buys an old tenement where many elderly and poor people live at modest rents. He tries to force them out so that he can remodel the buildings and rent one-bedroom apartments to people who earn high salaries and can afford to pay more than a thousand dollars a month for rent. Art galleries are moving in. Some newcomers keep trying to rename the neighborhood the East Village, probably hoping to make it sound as glamorous as Greenwich Village, which has a romantic past as the hangout of poets, painters, and playwrights. However, a group of people who have lived in the neighborhood for a long time are trying to maintain the community for all kinds of people.

BAGELS, BORSCHT, OR BISCOTTI?

BY MEG GREENE

As you stroll through New York's many neighborhoods, you will find street vendors, small cafés, and expensive restaurants where you can sample foods from around the world.

In Manhattan's Little Italy and in Bensonhurst in Brooklyn, you will find pastries such as cannolis and peasant pie. Restaurants offer a variety of Italian dishes: gnocchi (dumplings), calzones, and spaghetti. For dessert, you can enjoy an espresso with fresh fruit and spumoni.

The noodle shops and restaurants of Manhattan's Chinatown, the Flushing section of Queens, and Sunset Boulevard in Brooklyn display the many styles of Chinese cooking, from spicy Sichuan to mild Cantonese. In grocery stores, you can buy exotic ingredients such as gingerroot, bok choy, and fresh chicken feet to prepare your own meals at home.

The Lower East Side offers everything from Jewish delicatessens to restaurants featuring Greek moussaka, Puerto Rican *bacalos* (codfish), German sauerbraten, and Russian borscht. Many Jewish markets in the Borough Park section of Brooklyn sell smoked fish, bagels, and various "kosher" pastries, breads, and meats. (Kosher foods are prepared under a rabbi's supervision according to the rules of the Jewish faith.)

Uptown in Harlem or in the Bedford-Stuyvesant section of Brooklyn, you can eat "soul food" such as greens, barbecued ribs, and corn bread, which originated among African Americans living in the South. Restaurants that serve Jamaican, Haitian, and African dishes add variety to Harlem's culinary choices.

Street vendors are everywhere. The pizza, pickles, knish (dough stuffed with potato, meat, or cheese, then baked or fried), sausage and peppers, egg rolls, *cuchifritos* (fried pork), and hot dogs that they sell will satisfy even the most stubborn craving.

A NEW YORK MENU

THE ORIGINAL NEW YORK EGG CREAM

BY CHRISTINA MIERAU

YOU NEED
2 tablespoons chocolate syrup
1/4 cup cold milk
cold seltzer, club soda, or carbonated water
measuring cup and spoon, tall glass, straw, long-handled spoon

Seated at the counter of Joe's Bronx neighborhood candy store on high, red-padded stools, my friends and I would watch as Joe made one of his most popular fountain treats. He would pump two squirts of chocolate syrup into a tall glass and add a splash of cold milk. Then, holding the glass under the spout of a gleaming, goose-necked fountain, he would spritz it with chilled effervescent seltzer. The result was a thirst-quenching chocolate drink topped with a frothy head of white foam. Sipped through a straw and accompanied by a thick, salty pretzel, this classic concoction has been enjoyed by generations of New Yorkers.

No one is certain who invented the egg cream or chose its unusual name. (A New York egg cream contains neither eggs nor cream.) Historians speculate that the first egg cream was made at one of New York City's many soda fountains, which had become popular gathering spots during the temperance movement in the 1890s. According to Joe, the egg cream got its name because its frosty foam resembles the whipped egg whites used to top a meringue pie.

You can re-create a bit of the Big Apple's history in your own kitchen with a few simple ingredients and this recipe for the original New York egg cream.

1. Spoon the chocolate syrup into the glass.
2. Pour the milk over the syrup. Do not stir!
3. Fill the glass with cold seltzer.
4. Now stir. A creamy white foam will rise to the top of the glass.
5. Slip in the straw and enjoy your original New York egg cream.

★ For variety, add a scoop of vanilla ice cream or frozen yogurt, and you'll have a New York "black and white"!

LONGEVITY NOODLES
● ● ● ● ● ● ● ● ● ● ●
BY EILEEN YIN-FEI LO

So often in China, we eat the "symbols" as well as the food. When I was a girl growing up in Sun Tak, a suburb of Canton, we ate lotus root, believing that its texture with many holes meant that our minds would be open to new ideas. Oranges were for life's sweetness, grapefruit for abundance, peanuts for births, broccoli for youth, and steamed rice cakes for recurring life, because rice is a crop that recurs several times each year.

But nothing was more important at the table than noodles, which are considered key symbols of longevity. On every birthday, we *had* to have noodles, long and uncut. The longer the noodles, the longer life would be. In fact, great care was taken to see that no noodles were broken or cut in the boiling process. Only after a mounded platter of noodles had been presented to the table would they be cut and served in bowls.

In China, the tradition of noodle making is quite old. The Chinese were making noodles as far back as the Han dynasty, in 200 B.C., when noodles, breads, and buns were referred to as "grain food." Originally, noodles were made by cutting strands from large sheets of dough. Later came the practice of tossing lengths of dough into the air, over and over, until strands of thin noodles emerged. Called "beards of the dragon," the strands were quickly fried so that they looked like a mass of crinkly hair.

People throughout China eat noodles, generally called *mein*, boiled, fried, in soups, and stirred with vegetables, meats, and even fruits. There are different forms of noodles. For example, in southern China, in Fujian, spaghetti-like thin noodles are called *mi;* even thinner ones, like vermicelli, are *mi sua;* and wide, flat noodles are *kue thiau.*

When a person grows older, perhaps on one's sixtieth birthday, instead of noodles he or she is served a steamed-dough bun filled with sweet lotus seed paste and shaped like a peach. It is called "noodle food" and carries the same good luck as a platter of noodles.

This noodle preparation is from Sichuan, where hot peppers are used in many meals.

1. In the pot, bring the water to a boil. Add the noodles and stir. Cook for 1 1/2 minutes, or until al dente. Run cold water into the pot and drain the noodles. Repeat twice more.

2. Place the drained noodles in a bowl and toss with the sesame oil. Refrigerate, uncovered, for 1 hour.

3. In another bowl, combine the sesame seed paste, peanut but-

---

YOU NEED

8 cups water

8 ounces fresh noodles, such as thin spaghetti

1 1/2 tablespoons sesame oil

1 teaspoon sesame seed paste

3 tablespoons peanut butter

2 teaspoons white vinegar

2 tablespoons soy sauce

1 1/4 teaspoons red pepper flakes

1 tablespoon sugar

pinch of white pepper

2 tablespoons finely sliced scallions

2 sprigs coriander, broken into pieces

large pot, measuring cups and spoons, wooden spoon, colander, 2 mixing bowls, serving dish

---

ter, vinegar, soy sauce, red pepper flakes, sugar, white pepper, and scallions. Mix well.

4. Toss the noodles with the sesame sauce, place in the serving dish, garnish with the coriander, and serve. Serves 4 to 6.

Recipe adapted from *From the Earth: Chinese Vegetarian Cooking* by Eileen Yin-Fei Lo. Copyright © 1995 by Macmillan Publishing, New York.

TASTY TIRAMISÚ

BY DEANNA F. COOK

Are you looking for a little lift, Italian style? Take a bite of the Italian dessert *tiramisú* (tear-ah-me-sue). Translated, the name means "pick-me-up." It's so creamy and rich, it will pep up just about anyone!

Although tiramisú is no more than fifty years old, it is very popular in many Italian American restaurants — especially the fancy ones. It was first made in Venice, but its delicious taste has caught on here, too.

Why is it so popular? Tiramisú is layered with delicate ladyfingers (small, oval sponge cakes) and a sweetened Italian dessert cheese called mascarpone. Grated chocolate tops it all off. Plus, tiramisú is so easy to make, you don't even have to bake it!

1. Beat the egg yolks with the sugar. Add the vanilla and mascarpone or cream cheese and whipping cream. Beat until the mixture is fluffy and smooth.

2. Line the bottom of the pan with half the ladyfingers. Sprinkle the coffee on top.

3. Cover the ladyfingers with half the cheese mixture. Sprinkle half the grated chocolate over the cheese.

4. Add another layer of ladyfingers and the rest of the cheese mixture. Top it off with the remaining chocolate.

5. Refrigerate the tiramisú for at least 2 hours. Cut it into 6 pieces and serve. If you would like to be like the Italians, sip a little coffee on the side. (Add lots of warm milk if coffee tastes too strong to you.)

*Tiramisú also can be made in sundae glasses or individual glass dishes.

BOOKS TO READ

The Statue of Liberty *by Leonard Everett Fisher* (New York: Holiday House, 1985) combines historical photographs with the author's own illustrations to tell the story of the famous statue. Grades 4 to 9.

Immigrant Kids *by Russell Freedman* (New York: E.P. Dutton, 1980) explores the lives of immigrant children in the late 1800s and early 1900s through text and photographs, including many by Jacob Riis. Grades 3 to 5.

In the Year of the Boar and Jackie Robinson *by Bette Bao Lord* (New York: HarperCollins, 1986) tells the story of a young immigrant from China who has trouble adjusting to her new culture until she discovers America's pastime — baseball! Grades 3 to 5.

...If Your Name Was Changed at Ellis Island *by Ellen Levine* (New York: Scholastic, 1994) answers questions about the island and its history with interesting details, including quotes from children and adults who came through Ellis Island. Grades 3 to 5.

MORE MEDIA

Island of Hope, Island of Tears. This half-hour black-and-white film, available on video, tells the history of Ellis Island using interviews and photographs of immigrants who passed through its gates. Contact Ellis Island Immigration Museum: (212) 344-0996.

The Making of Liberty (1986). A history of the statue from its origin in France to its centennial celebration. Contact the museum shop: (212) 363-3180.

PLACES TO VISIT

Statue of Liberty. You can take a ferry to the famous statue on Liberty Island and then take the stairs (354 of them) to the statue's crown. An elevator goes to the top of the ten-story pedestal, where exhibits illustrate the statue's history and videos show the view from the top.

Ellis Island Immigration Museum. Exhibits describe the history of Ellis Island and the story of immigration to America from the first immigrants to the present day. The American Immigrant Wall of Honor lists the names of more than 420,000 American immigrants.

Lower East Side Tenement Museum. Here you can tour historic tenement apartments and view exhibits about immigrant life.

Museum of Chinese in the Americas. Art, photographs, and artifacts tell the story of Chinese immigration and the Chinese American experience.

alexander hamilton was born on St. Kitts...

Famous New Yorkers

ALEXANDER HAMILTON, THOMAS NAST, ALFRED STIEGLITZ, LANGSTON Hughes, Eleanor Roosevelt, Shirley Chisholm, Ed Koch. What do all these people have in common? They are all New Yorkers. Some lived long ago. Some live here today. But these people and many others are part of the history of this great city.

Alexander and Betsy Hamilton lived here at the very beginning of the United States. Alexander Hamilton helped to write the Constitution, the plan of government for the United States. You can watch the parade in New York celebrating the ratification, or approval, of the Constitution. With Hamilton's five children, watch for the float that honored their father — a ship called the *Hamilton.*

New York has always been home to writers. Meet Walt Whitman, who wrote for many of the city's newspapers. He was also one of our country's best-known poets. Another famous New York poet was Langston Hughes, who wrote about the lives of African Americans. His poem "Stars" will take you to a quiet night in Harlem.

You may never have heard of Thomas Nast, but he played a big role in the election of a number of presidents. A look at some of his cartoons will help you understand why.

A president of the United States was born right here in New York City. Theodore Roosevelt was often sick as a child, but he worked to make himself strong and grew up to be a police commissioner, soldier, vice president, and president.

Alfred Stieglitz and James Van DerZee were both photographers in New York. A look at their photographs will show you two different views of our city.

Fiorello La Guardia was mayor of New York for twelve years. Find out why one of the country's busiest airports is named for him.

Eleanor Roosevelt was married to Franklin Roosevelt, who was governor of New York and president of the United States. Take the train with her from Albany when she comes to New York to teach. After her husband died, she returned to live in the city and work at the United Nations.

New Yorkers have been first in many things. You will meet Shirley Chisholm, the first African American woman ever elected to Congress. You will also meet many other New Yorkers who have made this such a special place to live.

Learn how to take pictures on pages 162–163 so that you can take your own photographs of New Yorkers.

A Ship Called the *Hamilton*

BY VIRGINIA CALKINS

I t was July 23, 1788, and New York City was having a big parade. The Constitution of the United States had finally been ratified by ten states, and the people of New York wanted to celebrate.

Caught up in the excitement were Philip, Angelica, and Alexander, the natural children of Alexander and Betsy Hamilton. Fanny Antil, the orphan whom the Hamiltons had adopted, was excited, too. Baby James was only four months old, a bit too young to understand. The children waited impatiently for the parade to begin. Suddenly they heard the boom of a cannon. That was the starting signal.

> Hamilton believed that it was extremely important that New York join the Union.

A group of trumpeters led the parade. Then came artillerymen pulling a large cannon. Suddenly Philip exclaimed, "Look, everybody!" Coming toward them was a huge float pulled by ten white horses. The float was a model of a ship, a thirty-two-gun frigate. It had been constructed by shipbuilders and was twenty-seven feet long, large enough for a crew of thirty plus their officers.

As the float came closer, Angelica noticed something familiar about the figurehead at the front of the ship. "That looks like Papa," she said, raising her voice to make herself heard above the cheers of the crowd.

"Yes, child, the figurehead was

carved to look like your father," Mrs. Hamilton said. "The banner says that the ship is named the *Hamilton*."

Philip gave her a puzzled look. "Why did they name it after Father?" he asked.

"The people of New York are grateful to your father for the work he has done for the Constitution," his mother replied. "Remember when he was in Philadelphia last summer?"

Philip nodded. He remembered well.

"He was helping to write the Constitution then," Mrs. Hamilton said. "And remember last winter when he stayed up late night after night writing *The Federalist Papers*? Your father, Mr. Madison, and Mr. Jay wrote those papers to help people understand the Constitution and urge them to support it."

"I wish Father was here," Philip said with a sigh.

"I wish he was, too," his mother replied. "But your father is needed in Poughkeepsie. The state of New York is having a convention to decide whether it will ratify the Constitution, and your father is a delegate."

"Here comes another ship," little Alexander shouted.

This ship was made by sail mak-ers and named the *New Constitution*. A carved figure of Alexander Hamilton stood on its deck, with papers representing the new Constitution in his right hand and the Articles of Confederation in his left. This was to indicate the change from the Articles of Confederation to the Constitution.

More floats followed. Angelica and Fanny liked the one that featured a beautiful garland of artificial flowers. Three of the flowers were drooping, and Mrs. Hamilton explained that they represented the three states (including New York) that had not yet ratified the Constitution.

The parade continued, with marching bands, tradesmen and merchants, doctors, professors, and public officials. Ten law students carried the ten state ratifications. Three officials carried the new Constitution. More than five thousand people participated in the parade.

Eighty miles away in Poughkeepsie, Alexander Hamilton was fighting for ratification. When the convention had begun on June 17, only nineteen of the sixty-five delegates favored ratification. The leaders of the opposition were Governor George Clinton, who was the chairman of the convention, and Melancton Smith, a great debater. Hamilton believed that it was extremely important that New York join the Union. Besides being centrally located geographically, it also was a center of trade and commerce. How could he win over his opponents?

First he persuaded the delegates to debate the Constitution clause by clause, thus taking up time until he heard from New Hampshire or Virginia. At that point, eight states had ratified; another would mean that the Constitution would go into effect, with or without New York. Hamilton hoped that another ratification would convince some of the delegates to switch sides.

Suddenly he heard hoof beats. An express rider brought news that on June 21 New Hampshire had ratified the Constitution. The United States of America had been born!

Still the Antifederalists would not give in. On July 2, a messenger arrived from James Madison. Virginia had ratified! With this large state in the Union, it would be difficult for New York to stand alone.

Word reached Poughkeepsie about the parade being planned in New York City. There were rumors that the city might secede from the state if the convention failed to ratify. Finally, on July 26, New York ratified the Constitution with a recommendation for a Bill of Rights and other amendments. The vote was 30 to 27.

Alexander Hamilton returned to his family a tired but happy man. Proudly, he showed the ratification document to Betsy and the children. The children were impressed, but they really wanted to tell their father about the parade.

"It was tremendous," Philip related. "There was a ship called the *Hamilton.*"

His father picked up the ratification papers and moved toward the door. "I must bring this document to the Continental Congress at the City Hall," he said. "But I will return soon, and you can tell me about the parade. I want to hear everything, particularly about that ship called the *Hamilton!*"

Betsy Schuyler
Hamilton

BY JEANNE CONTE

Painted in 1787 by Ralph Earl, this is probably the only portrait of Betsy Schuyler Hamilton done during her lifetime.

lizabeth Schuyler was "most unmercifully handsome," according to Alexander Hamilton, who confided that "by some odd contrivance or other,...[she] has found the secret of interesting me in everything that concerns her." A visitor once described her as a "brunette with the most good natured, dark, lovely eyes...which threw a beam of good temper and benevolence over her entire countenance."

Who was this young lady who captured the heart of the dashing young Colonel Hamilton? Alternately called Betsy and Eliza by those close to her, Elizabeth Schuyler was born on August 9, 1757, one of General and Mrs. Philip Schuyler's large family. The Schuylers lived in a mansion in Albany, New York, where they entertained many prominent visitors such as George Washington, Benjamin

Franklin, and even General John Burgoyne, who stayed there as a prisoner-guest after his defeat by General Schuyler at the Battle of Saratoga.

Her father, a descendant of New Amsterdam's earliest settlers, served as a captain in the French and Indian War and as a major general in the Revolutionary War. He was prominent in the Continental Congress and one of New York's first U.S. senators.

Betsy's and Alexander's courtship began in Morristown, New Jersey, while Betsy was visiting a relative near General George Washington's winter quarters.* Their marriage on December 14, 1780, was a gala event at which the guests "supped a beef...dinner." Hamilton was enthusiastically received into the Schuyler family, as Betsy's father noted, "Alexander Hamilton did honor to the Schuyler family in marrying Betsy." The two men enjoyed a life-long friendship.

Not long after the war ended in 1781, Betsy gave birth to the Hamiltons' first son, Philip. "How entirely domestic I am growing," Alexander wrote to a friend. "I sigh for nothing

• •
*This was during the winter months of 1779–1780, when Washington's winter quarters were in Morristown.

but the company of my wife and baby." Betsy and Alexander had seven more children. Betsy also founded a home for orphans and contributed generously to charities throughout their married life.

While her husband alternately practiced law and served in public office, Betsy was his constant companion and helpmate. She sat up late at night listening to his ideas or recopying his writings. "Had she been any other than she was, despite all his genious [sic] and force of character, Hamilton could never have attained the place that he did," wrote their grandson and biographer, Dr. A.M. Hamilton.

"I distinctly recollect the scene at breakfast," son James described in 1797. "Mother...at the head of the table with a napkin in her lap, cutting slices of bread while the younger boys...read in turn a chapter from the Bible." On Sundays, the family attended services at Trinity Church on Wall Street and then strolled together down Broadway to their home.

One can only imagine Betsy's sadness when in 1801, Philip died in a duel defending his father's honor. Like his father three years later, Philip had refused to fire the first shot, on moral grounds. His sister Angelica never recovered from her brother's death. After suffering his own mortal wound in 1804, Alexander murmured, "Let the event be gradually broken to her [Betsy], but give her hope." Betsy came with her seven children, and although she was told he was merely having "spasms," she knew he would die.

In Alexander's last letter to his wife, he wrote, "The scruples of a Christian have determined me to expose my own life to any extent rather than subject myself to the guilt of taking the life of another.... You had rather I die innocent than live guilty.... Adieu, my darling, darling wife."

Within months of Alexander's death, Betsy's parents also died. Widowed at forty-seven, with seven children (one insane) and a staggering fifty-five thousand dollars in debts, Betsy spent the remaining years of her life in an attempt to preserve her husband's honor. She filed a lawsuit to protect her husband's name and searched diligently for an adequate biographer. Ultimately, her son John and grandson A.M. Hamilton filled that role.

"Never forget that my husband made your government!" Betsy once told a distinguished caller. She maintained that dignity and loyalty to her husband until her death at age ninety-seven.

Walt Whitman, Journalist

BY BARBARA HALL

t is the summer of 1839, and for two hours a tall young man has been stretched out under an apple tree, dozing as if the world is his apple and clocks do not exist. A "printer's devil" — a messenger sent by newspaper publisher James J. Brenton — approaches the sleeping man and jostles him awake. The young man, dressed simply in black, slowly trails the messenger back to the *Long Island Democrat* press. The man is Walt Whitman, who in his own good time will become one of the great journalists of his day.

Dozens of newspapers were published in and around New York City during the mid-1800s. For about thirty years beginning when he was twelve years old, Whitman wrote for many of them, including the *Brooklyn Daily Eagle, Brooklyn Times, Brooklyn Standard, Brooklyn Advertizer, Brooklyn Evening Post, New York Times, New York Post, Long Island Democrat, Long Island Patriot, Long Island Farmer, Evening Signal, Evening Tattler, Aurora, Sun, Long Island Star, New Mirror, Statesman, Weekly Freeman,* and *New World.* He also wrote briefly for the New Orleans *Crescent* in Louisiana.

One of his biographers, Henry Seidel Canby, says Whitman was "a roving reporter such as seldom comes out of a newspaper office." He was a free spirit, and he was full of curiosity, an important journalistic trait. He hated what he saw as injustice and championed the common people. He used language as if it flowed like music, and he loved life.

What makes a journalist? For

Whitman, it might have been an incident he saw at age ten — the explosion of the steam frigate *Fulton* that killed forty to fifty people — which he later described in exact detail. Or maybe it was the influence of William Hartshorne, the quiet, kindly *Long Island Patriot* newsman who taught a twelve-year-old boy to set type and told wonderful stories about George Washington and Thomas Jefferson, whom he had known. Whatever it was, Whitman was a journalist long before he became a celebrated poet.

For Whitman, journalism was education and more. Schools in Long Island and Brooklyn did not teach him what newspapers would. He learned to spell and punctuate sentences by setting type, in effect feeling the words with his hands. Once on the *Patriot* staff, he began traveling to New York City, where the world of books, theater, art, politics, and people opened before him.

The *Patriot*'s motto was "The right of the people to rule in every case." Like most newspapers in the region, it was a political paper, a mouthpiece for Tammany Hall, which at that time was

This engraving of Walt Whitman appeared in the first edition of Leaves of Grass, his classic poem, in 1855.

a powerful local branch of the Democratic party. Whitman's support of the Democrats (but not always of Tammany) and his faith in the masses may have been born at the *Patriot*.

While his journalism career began with the *Patriot*, Whitman soon developed a habit of newspaper hopping. For a short time between papers, he taught school in a series of one-room schoolhouses on Long Island. While teaching there, he wrote a series of articles, called "Sun-Down Papers from the Desk of a School-Master," that was published by the *Long Island Democrat*. This teaching experience would resurface later as he neared the peak of his journalism career.

At age twenty-six, he became a special correspondent for the *Long Island Star*. By now he knew the territory and the trade. Before joining the *Star*, he had written page one stories about New York City's cast of characters — butchers, firemen, horse-car drivers, and others. As an editor at one paper, he had quoted Homer and Shakespeare in his pleas for better treatment of the poor and the helpless, and he had crossed swords with the city's leading politicians and publishers. "Editing a daily paper, to be sure, is arduous employment," he wrote during those years, "...but it is a delight."

While working on the *Star,* he remembered his year of teaching and decided to "clean up" Brooklyn's schools. He criticized the "miserable slovenliness in the plan of appointing [Brooklyn] teachers." He declared that "the instructor who uses the lash in his school at all, is unworthy to hold the power he does." (Lashing often was used to enforce classroom discipline.) He also wrote on other subjects, and one story unexpectedly brought him fame as a journalist.

Brooklynite William B. Marsh died on February 26, 1846, leaving his widow and children poverty-stricken. Characteristically openhearted, Whitman came to their rescue. His call for financial help was printed in the *Star,* and readers responded with generosity.

William Marsh had been editor of the *Brooklyn Daily Eagle,* a young but respected daily. The *Daily Eagle*'s owner heard about Whitman's deed, and within a week the *Daily Eagle* had a new editor: Walt Whitman.

At the *Daily Eagle,* Whitman opposed capital punishment and expressed shock at poor working conditions for the city's "sewing-women."

He led a successful crusade for more churches in Brooklyn and warned that bitter division between the North and South on the slavery issue could destroy the nation. As his thoughtfulness grew at the *Daily Eagle,* so did his talent for communicating his thoughts. While he still chased fires and hobnobbed with city politicians, it became more and more evident that here was a writer to be reckoned with. He led the *Daily Eagle* for two years but was then fired for his belief that slavery should be kept out of Kansas, a stand that went against that of his boss.

While he was out of work, Whitman met a man named J.E. McClure, who, with a partner, happened to be starting a journal in New Orleans. Would Whitman be interested in joining the enterprise? Within two weeks, Whitman and his brother Jeff were in Louisiana. Whitman worked for the New Orleans *Crescent* for only three months and soon was back in New York, hopping newspapers but now also seriously writing poetry.

Whitman made one more important stop on his journey from journalist to poet. The Civil War he had feared finally came. In 1862, Whitman left

New York to view the southern battle-fields. He went directly to Fredericks-burg, Virginia, then stopped in Washington, D.C., on his return. Deeply moved by the thousands of dying and wounded soldiers, he stayed in Washington, working at the Bureau of Indian Affairs and caring for the sick and wounded in his free time. While in Washington, he described the horrors of war in reports that were published in the *New York Times* and other city papers.

As a journalist, Walt Whitman is best remembered for matching strong words with strong feelings, always showing character and courage in his work. As a poet, he later would express the same attitude toward people, free-dom, and democracy.

From the Pen of Walt Whitman

. . . .

COMPILED BY DELORIS SELINSKY

I am a man who, sauntering along
without fully stopping, turns a casu-
al look upon you and then averts his
face,
Leaving it to you to prove and define it,
Expecting the main things from you.
(from "Poets to Come")

. . . .

I am the poet of the woman the same
as the man,
And I say it is as great to be a woman
as to be a man,
And I say there is nothing greater than
the mother of men.
(from "Song of Myself")

. . . .

To have great poets, there must be
great audiences, too.
(from "Ventures, On an Old Theme")

To me every hour of the light and dark
is a miracle,
Every cubic inch of space is a miracle,
Every square yard of the surface of the
earth is spread with the same,
Every foot of the interior swarms with
the same.
(from "Miracles")

. . . .

I dream'd in a dream I saw a city invin-
cible to the attacks of the whole of
the rest of the earth,
I dream'd that was the new city of
Friends.
(from "I Dream'd in a Dream")

. . . .

Love like the light silently wrapping all.
(from "Song of the Universal")

A child said What is the grass? fetching
   it to me with full hands,
How could I answer the child? I do not
   know what it is any more than he.
                    (from "Song of Myself")

• • • • • • • • • • •

He [Abraham Lincoln] leaves for America's history and biography, so far, not
only its most dramatic reminiscence —
he leaves, in my opinion, the greatest,
best, most characteristic, artistic,
moral personality. Not but that he had
faults, and show'd them in the Presidency; but honesty, goodness, shrewd-
ness, conscience, and (a new virtue,
unknown to other lands, and hardly
yet really known here, but the foundation and tie of all, as the future will
grandly develop,) Unionism, in its
truest and amplest sense, form'd the
hard-pan of his character. These he
seal'd with his life.
                    (from Specimen Days)

• • • • • • • • • • •

A noiseless patient spider,
I mark'd where on a little promontory it
   stood isolated,
Mark'd how to explore the vacant vast
   surrounding,
It launch'd forth filament, filament,
   filament out of itself,

Ever unreeling them, ever tirelessly
   speeding them.
             (from "A Noiseless Patient Spider")

• • • • • • • • • • •

Political democracy, as it exists and
practically works in America, with all
its threatening evils, supplies a train-
ing-school for making first-class men.
It is life's gymnasium, not of good only,
but of all.
                    (from Democratic Vistas)

• • • • • • • • • • •

There was a child went forth every day,
And the first object he look'd upon,
   that object he became,
And that object became part of him for
   the day or a certain part of the day,
Or for many years or stretching cycles
   of years.
       (from "There Was a Child Went Forth")

• • • • • • • • • • •

I hear America singing, the varied
   carols I hear....
Each singing what belongs to him or
   her and to none else.
                (from "I Hear America Singing")

Thomas Nast: Maker of Presidents

BY PAULINE C. BARTEL

One picture is worth a thousand words. This saying holds especially true for the father of American political cartooning. He drew the Democratic donkey and the Republican elephant. His sharp pencil also had the power to help elect presidents. His name is Thomas Nast.

Tom was born in Landau, Germany, on September 27, 1840. He came to America with his family when he was six years old. Tom attended New York City public schools, but he was not interested in grammar or arithmetic. He loved to draw. "Go finish your picture," a teacher told him. "You will never learn to read or figure." Tom left school when he was accepted to the Academy of Design, where he studied art.

When Tom was fifteen, he applied for a job at the magazine *Leslie's Weekly.* The publisher, Frank Leslie, was so impressed with Tom's drawing ability that he hired him as an illustrator. Tom's salary was four dollars a week. He worked at *Leslie's Weekly* for three years.

When the Civil War broke out, Tom became a war reporter on the staff of *Harper's Weekly Magazine.* The war was a great theme for the young artist. His drawings of battle scenes, full of spirit and patriotism, attracted the country's attention. President Lincoln said, "Thomas Nast has been our best recruiting sergeant."

Tom played an important role in President Lincoln's reelection. In 1864, the war was not going well for the North. Many people blamed Lincoln. They were tired of the war. The

Democratic candidate, General George B. McClellan, promised peace at any price. Lincoln didn't think he had a chance to be reelected. In August, he wrote, "It seems exceedingly probable that this administration will not be reelected." But he had not counted on the support of Thomas Nast. Tom drew cartoons showing McClellan as a man who would compromise with the South. The cartoons helped President Lincoln win reelection.

When the war ended, Tom continued to draw cartoons of political figures. He was such an expert in this art that he rarely needed to label any of his subjects, for they were recognized immediately. The power of Tom's drawings also came from their size. He drew cover drawings for *Harper's,* as well as full and double-page cartoons.

Tom liked having his wife read to him while he drew. Sarah would read from newspapers and books of fiction. When she was busy, Tom hired college students at one dollar an hour. They read from the classics, history, and science books.

In the 1868 presidential election, General Ulysses S. Grant, a Republican, ran against the Democrat Horatio Seymour. Grant was Tom's idol. In this campaign, Tom's cartoons accused the Democrats of trying to fight the Civil War again. "Two things elected me," war hero Grant later said, "the sword of Sheridan and the pencil of Thomas Nast."

Tom's pencil created the donkey symbol of the Democratic party. The donkey was based on a creature in Aesop's fable "The Sick Lion." In that fable, a lion lies dying in his cave. The other animals gather around him and notice he is helpless. Even the donkey feels safe, so he kicks the lion.

The donkey first appeared in a cartoon in January of 1870, after the death of Republican Edwin L. Stanton, who had been secretary of war in the cabinets of Lincoln and Johnson. The Democratic newspapers began attacking Stanton's reputation. Tom came to the rescue with his cartoon showing the newspapers (donkey) kicking the dead Stanton (lion).

Tom supported Grant when he ran for reelection in 1872. Opposing Grant was Horace Greeley, editor of the *New York Tribune.* Cartoons of Greeley showed he would do anything to beat Grant. Greeley's vice-presidential running mate was Governor Gratz Brown of Missouri. Tom did not have a photograph of Brown to use for drawing his cartoons, so he drew Brown as a tag

"WE ARE ON THE HOME STRETCH."—*New York Tribune*, October 9, 1872.

attached to the coattails of Greeley. Just before the election, Greeley made a speech and said his campaign was "on the home stretch." Tom used this idea. He drew a cartoon showing Greeley being carried off on a stretcher. Grant won reelection.

n 1874, the *New York Herald* thought that Grant would be running for a third term. They called him a dictator. Tom was a loyal Republican. To defend Grant, he borrowed another of Aesop's fables, "The Donkey in the Lion's Skin." In that fable, a donkey finds a lion's skin, puts it on, and frightens animals on his way to the village.

Tom's cartoon, "The Third Term Panic," was printed in November 1874. The *New York Herald* is the donkey frightening the other New York papers. The Republican party is the elephant about to fall into a pit. This was the first time the elephant appeared as the symbol of the party. The Republicans eventually adopted the elephant symbol. They said it showed their size and strength.

In the 1876 election, Republican

Rutherford B. Hayes ran against Samuel Tilden, in what was to be one of the most hotly contested elections in our history. Tom's cartoons backed Hayes, and he won by one electoral vote. Tom's cartoon of a wounded elephant showed the Republican party's close victory.

In that cartoon, the Democratic party is represented by a dead tiger. Tom used other animals, such as a fox and a wolf, to represent the party, but the Democrats liked the image of the donkey best and accepted the animal as their symbol. The donkey and elephant first appeared together in the 1879 cartoon "Stranger Things Have Happened."

The 1884 election was a turning point for Tom. The Republicans had nominated James G. Blaine, former speaker of the House of Representatives. Blaine was accused of having used his office for personal gain. "Speaking for myself," Tom said, "I positively decline to support Blaine, either directly or indirectly even if the Democrats should nominate

the Devil himself."

The Democrats nominated Grover Cleveland, and Tom supported him.

THE THIRD-TERM PANIC.

Harper's went along with his choice. This was the first time in twenty-five years that the magazine had backed a Democrat. Tom and *Harper's* came under fire for their choice, but Tom would not change his mind. One of his cartoons showed Blaine as a "magnetic candidate" with his head on a barrel of campaign money. This election was very close, but Cleveland won. And Thomas Nast had become known as a maker of presidents.

The Cyclone Touches Down

BY JOAN HUNT

"ho's the dude?" asked New York assemblyman John Walsh as the 1882 session of the state legislature began. Young Theodore Roosevelt, wearing a silk hat and pince-nez and carrying a gold-headed cane, flashed a smile. It was the smile of a bulldog who growled at every issue and attacked corrupt politics and politicians.

Roosevelt's maiden speech demanded that a state supreme court justice be impeached for giving judicial favors to wealthy associates. Combining forces with a few honest state legislators, he opened a much-publicized investigation, which supported his accusations. Soon people began to call Roosevelt "the cyclone assemblyman."

Following a brief spell in North Dakota, he continued his political career. A third-place finish in New York's mayoral race in 1886 was followed three years later by an appointment by President Benjamin Harrison as chairman of the Civil Service Commission. It was a job that nobody else wanted. Roosevelt constantly butted heads with the powerful politician makers in Washington. He substituted their spoils system of awarding government jobs to political friends with a well-organized program that tested candidates for their ability to do the work.

President Harrison observed that

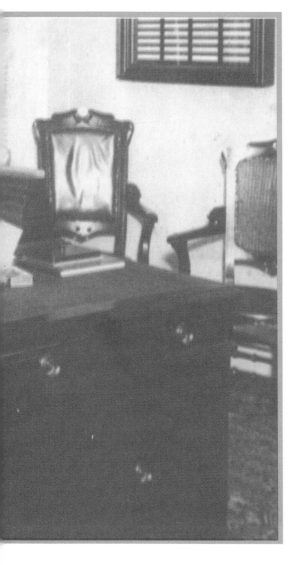

As New York City police commissioner, Theodore Roosevelt, known as the "reform commissioner," literally tore through his work.

Roosevelt "wanted to put an end to all the evil in the world between sunrise and sunset." Although Roosevelt knew that he was creating powerful enemies in politics, he insisted that it was better to be thrown out of office for doing a good job than to keep it by doing a bad one.

In 1895, he took a new post guaranteed to make him even more enemies. As president of the New York City Police Commission, he had control over law enforcement, the Board of Health, and a corrupt police department. He wasted little time, forcing the chief of police to resign.

Commissioner Roosevelt prowled the streets at night, making sure that his officers were on duty. He awarded medals for special service, promoting those who worked hard and could pass a competitive examination. No longer would policemen "buy" their jobs or accept bribes.

After a tour of the city's tenements, Roosevelt strengthened inspection standards. He also enforced the law forbidding Sunday alcohol sales, which angered saloonkeepers, brewers, and influence peddlers. Criminals, crooked politicians, and corporate lobbyists despised him. Warned that he was slitting his political throat, Roo-

sevelt replied that if he thought about his political career, he would start being careful and stop being effective.

Roosevelt became assistant secretary of the Navy in 1897. In that position, he bought ships, hired recruits, and trained them to use their weapons. Because of his preparedness, the Navy was not taken by surprise when the United States went to war to free Cuba from Spanish rule. Leaving his post, he enlisted in the Army, leading the Rough Riders in the Spanish-American War.

He returned from Cuba a hero. Meanwhile, the scandal-ridden Republican party was looking for a new image. Thomas Platt, boss of the New York Republican political machine, encouraged him to run for governor, even though Platt was afraid that he would not be able to control Roosevelt. Promising that he would rule by the Ten Commandments, Roosevelt won — and immediately confirmed Platt's fears.

Governor Roosevelt refused to appoint Platt's friends unless they were honest and qualified. He went over Platt's head to pass a bill taxing corporations on certain profits. The Department of Public Works, charitable and penal institutions, and the insurance and banking industries all felt the bite of Roosevelt's reform measures. Platt could not wait to get rid of him.

President William McKinley needed a new running mate in 1900, as his vice president, Garret A. Hobart, had died in office. It was easy for Platt to steer the nomination toward Roosevelt, who was enormously popular with the people. A loyal Republican, Roosevelt took the job even though he knew that it carried no weight.

Confident that Roosevelt was now out of the way, Platt relaxed. Mark Hanna of the Republican National Committee was not so comfortable with the move. "Don't any of you realize there's only one life between this madman and the White House?" he asked. Those prophetic words foretold changes that would dwarf Roosevelt's efforts in his middle years. The McKinley-Roosevelt team was elected. In 1901, McKinley was assassinated, and Roosevelt became president.

Alfred Stieglitz

· ·

BY HARRY S. STOUT AND DEBORAH H. DEFORD

Suppose you were to come to the dinner table one day and find it set with a special flower centerpiece. But what if the flower arrangement was in a copper kettle used for boiling water instead of a vase? Would it strike you as an odd or even wrong use of the kettle?

t probably would the first time you saw it. But maybe after the second or third time, you would like flowers in the kettle as much as (or more than) flowers in a vase. In fact, there might be flower arrangements you found interesting only because they were in that battered copper pot.

When photography first began in the mid-1800s, many people believed that it had one basic use. Just as you might think a kettle is good only for boiling water, these people believed a photograph was good only for capturing a likeness of people, a pretty scene, or an important event. It took a person with the imagination to see beyond the most obvious usefulness of pho-

tographs and the courage to do something different to consider the camera not only as a toy or a gadget but as an instrument for making art.

That person was Alfred Stieglitz, considered by many as the "Father of Modern Photography." More than any other American photographer of his age, Stieglitz took photography seriously and made people understand the camera as an artist's tool that was every bit as important as a painter's brush or a sculptor's chisel.

Stieglitz was born on New Year's

In his photograph *Winter — Fifth Avenue,* Alfred Stieglitz caught the busy avenue in an unusual moment.

Day, 1864, in the midst of the Civil War. As a child, Stieglitz showed signs of genius and independence, but none pointed directly to photography. Both of his parents encouraged his interest in art and sent him to the finest private and public schools in New York.

Soon after Stieglitz turned seventeen, his family went to Germany for several years. In Germany, he studied mechanical engineering, following his father's wishes. But he soon tired of it and moved on to the University of Berlin, where he took a course in photography that would change his life. Photographs fascinated him, "first as a toy, then as a passion, then as an obsession. I took to it as a musician takes to the piano or a painter to canvas," Stieglitz said.

Before long, Stieglitz had turned his dormitory room into a darkroom and was taking pictures zealously. Sometimes he would photograph a single object many times "to get it right." Eventually, his efforts won him a medal in photography that encouraged him on his future path.

When the Stieglitz family returned to New York, Stieglitz entered a photo-engraving business with his father's backing. But his interest was clearly not in business — he spent all his time and energy taking and developing pictures. When Stieglitz was not taking pictures himself, he was talking with a growing circle of friends who shared his passion for photography and wanted it taken seriously as an art.

But like using a kettle for a vase, the idea of using photography for making art was unfamiliar to most people and was not immediately accepted. Stieglitz tried several ways to help people get a fresh view of photography. One way he did this was to work on magazines dedicated to the serious study and exhibition of artistic photographs. These journals would teach other photographers to appreciate the art and skill involved in a good photograph. They also helped photographers recognize the difference between a simple snapshot and a photograph that had an important message or aimed for artistic excellence.

In addition to the magazines, Stieglitz also began a photography club and an art gallery in New York City. The club and gallery would become so famous that they would make New York the photography capital of America. His club, which began in 1902, was called Photo-Secession — a term showing Stieglitz's desire to break away from old methods of photography that borrowed too much from painters. Photo-Secession included many of Stieglitz's friends and fellow photographers, including his best friend, Edward Steichen.

I n 1905, Stieglitz and Steichen opened an art gallery at 291 Fifth Avenue, later known simply as 291. In 1907, Stieglitz added paintings and sculptures to his exhibits, later including the work of now famous modern European artists such as Matisse, Cézanne, and Picasso. 291 became a leading center of avant-garde art, introducing American audiences to artists who were revolutionizing the field of art. By exhibiting photographs alongside new works in painting and sculpture, Stieglitz also won new respect for photography.

Magazines, clubs, and the art gallery were all important means of promoting photography, but Stieglitz did not stop there. His most famous contribution to photography would be his own photographs. Unlike other photographers, Stieglitz recognized that photography could not simply imitate paintings of wealthy patrons or rural settings. He refused to "touch up" his negatives so the pictures would look brushed on, like a painting. Instead, he took the camera for what it was: an instrument that could catch glimpses of modern American society and tell its story in a unique way.

Modern America's story was that of the Industrial Revolution and the growth of cities like New York. While Stieglitz did not ignore portraits or nature, his main interest was New York City. His photographs tell of America's change from a society of small farms to one of modern cities. Nowhere is this theme captured better than in his picture *Winter — Fifth Avenue* (1893). It shows a horse-drawn carriage moving down modern Fifth Avenue in the midst of a swirling snowstorm. The photo captures what Stieglitz called his "sense of loneliness in my own country."

No paintings or sculptures tell modern America's story better or more artistically than the photographs of the Stieglitz circle. They proved that photography was more than a useful image recorder. It became the most important art form of the twentieth century.

James Van DerZee: Harlem's Photographer

BY BETH IRWIN KANE

As a little boy, James Van DerZee loved drawing and painting. But it seemed that no matter how hard he tried, the faces never turned out right. Then one day he saw an advertisement in a boys' magazine that offered a camera for selling twenty packages of sachet (perfumed powder). With a camera, James reasoned, his pictures would have to turn out right.

Selling the sachet was not easy, but James earned his camera. The day it arrived with its developing chemicals and glass plates was an exciting one, and James could hardly wait to begin. After reading the instructions carefully, James tried to take a picture. He tried over and over again, then realized sadly that the camera would never work. "It was just a cheap little box," he said later, "with a piece of broken eyeglass for a lens."

The nine-year-old was not about to give up. He got a job setting out plants and earned enough to buy himself a good camera. He turned his bedroom closet into a darkroom and began photographing his friends and neighbors. Most often he gave his pictures away, but some people insisted on paying him. When they did pay, James said that ten cents seemed a fair price. Today his photographs cost from four hundred to fifteen hundred dollars each.

In 1915, James was hired as a photographer's assistant. It was not long before customers began requesting James over the boss. In time, customers encouraged James to open his own studio in Harlem. This was an

This James Van DerZee photograph is titled *Couple, Harlem, 1932.*

exciting place to be in the 1920s and 1930s. Famous black entertainers flocked to Harlem's nightspots. Talented African American writers, poets, athletes, and politicians were part of what became known as the Harlem Renaissance (see pages 197–205). James photographed these famous men and women, as well as the not-so-famous people who lived there.

His advertisements read "James Van DerZee: Artist and Photographer."

He arranged lights and background to bring out a subject's best expression. If a photograph was not to his liking, he would fix it up with his retouching pencil or his etching knife. "The main thing," James said, "is to get the camera to see it the way you see it…. If it wasn't beautiful, why, I took out the unbeautifulness."

Sometimes James superimposed one picture on another to tell a story. This was called "multiple image technique." James had no idea that the technique had been used before. He just figured out how to use the technique and then did it. "When it came to photography," he said, "I can't recall ever trying to do something I couldn't do, but at the same time I was always trying to do better."

James photographed the people of Harlem for more than fifty years. Sadly, the golden days of the Harlem Renaissance disappeared with the Great Depression. Parts of Harlem became places of poverty and crime. James continued to work in Harlem, though his later years were devoted to restorations.

It was not until 1967 that the Harlem James knew and photographed was "discovered." James was eighty-three years old when a researcher named Reginald McGhee first contacted him. McGhee had been assigned to locate photographs for the Metropolitan Museum of Art's upcoming show "Harlem on My Mind." McGhee visited a number of photography studios in Harlem, and

in each he heard of an elderly photographer whom people fondly referred to as "the picture-takin' man."

McGhee made an appointment to meet James and to take a look at his photographs. As soon as he saw the pictures, about fifty thousand of them, he knew he had struck gold. James was a "master." Each one of his photographs had been signed and dated, with careful attention paid to its composition and finishing. James's photos had an artist's instinctive grasp of the principles of light, texture, contrast, and depth.

James's photographs — more than half a century of work — formed the nucleus of the Metropolitan Museum's show. Suddenly, James was a celebrity.

Today James Van DerZee's work is considered important not only for its technical excellence but also for its historical value. Without his photographs, the events of the Harlem Renaissance might have been lost forever. Above all, James's work is valued for its universal and raceless message of the beauty and the dignity of all people.

Fiorello La Guardia: The Fighting Flower

BY DIANA CHILDRESS

The name Fiorello means "little flower" in Italian, hardly a suitable name for a rambunctious Army brat who would one day be the mayor of New York City. But that is just what Fiorello La Guardia was when he was growing up in the 1880s and 1890s on the U.S. Army bases where his Italian immigrant father was a bandleader. Small for his age, with a shock of dark hair and dark eyes, young Fiorello was a scrapper who loved a good fight, regardless of the odds against him. Once, in a battle with a much taller boy, he stood on a chair, the better to hit him.

Fiorello also was smart, "a joy and a problem" to his teachers. He scolded one for making mistakes in math and refused to answer another for calling him FYE-o-rello instead of FEE-o-rello. As one teacher later recalled, "I knew he was bound to be someone important. He was not only stubborn about having his way, but he also knew what he was talking about. Everything interested him."

Young Fiorello cared deeply about oppression and injustice. He felt sympathy for injured Mexican railroad workers and hungry Indian children living near the Army barracks in Arizona Territory. He was appalled by the political corruption he read about in the newspapers. When President Grover Cleveland called out troops to

stop a railway strike in 1894 and several strikers were killed, Fiorello was angry that labor disputes could not be settled more peacefully.

Even as a boy, Fiorello liked to make speeches to his friends about solving these and other problems. He believed that "good people could eliminate bad people from public office." It was a goal he set out to accomplish.

The La Guardias moved back to Italy in 1898, but Fiorello returned to the United States in 1906, telling his widowed mother that he was ambitious to "be somebody and do something really worthwhile." He studied and practiced law, read the *Congressional Record* faithfully, and worked hard for the Republican party.

When La Guardia ran for Congress in 1914, few people took him seriously. But he campaigned hard, taking advantage of his knowledge of Italian and Yiddish, as well as English, to appeal to ethnic voters. When he came close to winning the election, the politicians took notice and appointed him deputy attorney general of New York. Two years later, he ran again

In 1946, Fiorello La Guardia waved farewell to his friends at City Hall, where he had served as mayor for twelve years.

and won, becoming the first Italian American to serve in the House of Representatives.

When the United States entered World War I the next year, Congressman La Guardia volunteered for military service. He trained fliers, flew bombing missions, and made speeches in Italy to win Italian support for the United States. He returned to Washington a hero decorated by King Victor Emmanuel III of Italy.

Fighting of a different kind came after the war. The political climate of the twenties was too conservative for many of the progressive laws La Guardia proposed. He protested against immigration quotas, denounced high food prices, and fought Prohibition. He spoke so often in the House that one observer said, "He never rises to speak — he bounces."

He had victories, too. He earned national acclaim for his labor legislation, particularly the Norris–La Guardia Act, which limited the use of strikebreaking methods such as those used by President Cleveland in 1894. In a congratulatory letter, black labor leader A. Philip Randolph hailed La Guardia as a leader of "all the oppressed groups in America."

When La Guardia lost his congressional seat in 1932, his fighting spirit did not flag. Liberal Republicans and Democrats opposed to the corrupt Tammany Hall political machine in New York City had organized the new Fusion party. La Guardia was not their first choice as mayoral candidate because his quarrelsome personality offended some of the new party's backers. But La Guardia persisted, gained their support, and became the first Italian American mayor of New York.

One of his campaign promises was to leave politics behind when he entered City Hall. To everyone's surprise, he kept it. He refused to reward campaign supporters with jobs, instead choosing experts to run the city.

He modernized New York, clearing slums to build low-cost housing, schools, parks, highways, bridges, and tunnels. He unified the subway and trolley companies into the most extensive transit network in the world. One of his pet projects, which critics called "Fiorello's Folly," was New York's first municipal airport, La Guardia Field, still one of the busiest airports in the country.

For twelve years, Mayor La Guardia brought his vigorous style of governing to New York. He kept such a close eye on everything that one official recalled, "It seemed as though the town had been invaded by an army of small, plump men in big hats; he was everywhere."

Upon La Guardia's death in 1947, President Harry Truman praised him as "incorruptible as the sun." Today the "Little Flower" is fondly remembered as a crusader for honest, caring, and fair public service.

Harlem Poet

. . . .

BY MILTON MELTZER

The subway train rushed madly through the tunnel as Langston Hughes counted off the numbered signs to 135th Street, where he got off. The platform was jammed with black people on their way to work. Lugging his heavy bag up the stairs, he came out on the corner of Lenox Avenue. It was a September morning in 1921. Nineteen-year-old Hughes stood there feeling good. But being there felt a little crazy, too, as if he had finally come home, though he had never been to Harlem before.

With a week to go before beginning classes at Columbia University, he got a room at the YMCA. That afternoon, he crossed the street to visit the Harlem Branch Library, where the librarians made him feel right at home. That night, he went into the Lincoln Theatre to hear a blues singer.

He spent the next few days mapping Harlem with his feet. The great dark expanse of this island within an island fascinated him. In 1921, Harlem ran from 125th Street north to 145th and from Madison Avenue to Eighth Avenue. Eighty thousand African Americans were packed into the long rows of tenements as the flood of southern blacks continued to roll north.

Hughes had begun to write poetry in high school in Cleveland. One of his teachers had introduced him to the work of American poets such as Carl Sandburg, Vachel Lindsay, and Robert Frost, all of whom were exploring new ways to create poetry. His teacher encouraged him to find his own lyric voice, and the school paper published some of his work.

Hughes found Columbia too big and too cold and the instructors too busy to bother with a black student who needed help. But he kept writing poems and sent several to *The Crisis,* a black magazine. It published one, which began, "I am a Negro / Black as the night is black / Black as the depths of my Africa." The readers liked the poem so much that *The Crisis* published more.

College did not seem right for Hughes, and he left after one year. After a year of working and writing poetry in New York, he found a job as a steward on a freighter bound for Africa. He was twenty-one now and on his own. As the ship made stops at ports along the western shore of Africa, he saw that blacks lived under white laws made abroad for the black colonies, laws that were enforced by whip and gun.

His next job on a freighter brought him to France. He left the ship to discover the Paris every young poet dreamed about. He worked in nightclubs as a doorman, dishwasher, and cook. Alone in his tiny room, he continued to write poetry, fitting the rhythms of jazz into the rhythm of words, and sent his poems off to New York. A magazine bought three of them for $24.50 — the first time he had ever been paid for writing. When he lost his job in Paris, he worked his way home on an American ship.

Back in Harlem, Hughes found himself among several black writers and artists and began friendships that would last. But he was penniless and could not find work. In early 1925, he moved to Washington, D.C., taking jobs in a laundry, as a clerk, and then as a bellman in a hotel. His big break came when the popular white poet Vachel Lindsay read Hughes's poems to a large audience, praising them highly. Overnight, newspapers across the country spread the story of this new poet.

It was the beginning of Hughes's fame but not his fortune. He won literary prizes, was published in many places, and found his way back to Harlem in 1925. There Carl Van Vechten, a widely known white writer who befriended many black artists, took Hughes's poems to a publisher, suggesting that they would make a good book. When Hughes's book *The Weary Blues* appeared in 1926, critics hailed it as powerful, warm, and lyrical.

Still, Hughes felt that his education was unfinished. He wanted to go

This drawing of a young Langston Hughes was done by Winold Reiss in the 1920s.

back to college "in order to be of more use to my race and America," he said. The oldest black school in the country, Lincoln University in Pennsylvania, admitted him. But how could he afford to go without a dime in his pocket? Amy Spingarn, a white woman who admired his poetry, offered to pay his way through Lincoln.

He spent summers in New York, working and immersing himself in Harlem life. All his artist friends were trying to find their roots and new ways to shape black life into art. Hughes experimented with forms derived from black culture. He voiced the spirit of the blues, of spirituals, folk ballads, and gospel songs. With a deceptive simplicity, he suggested the variety and complexity of the black experience. His pioneering use of blues forms and jazz rhythms would be the major innovation in the poetry of the Harlem Renaissance.

A second book of his poems came out in 1927. And soon after graduation from Lincoln, his novel *Not Without Laughter* appeared in 1930. Through its characters, he explored the challenges young blacks had to face in a racist society.

In 1929, the Great Depression hit the United States. Even with millions of people jobless and homeless, Hughes decided to try to make a living solely by writing. He made ends meet by traveling the country in an old car and giving readings of his poems at black schools, colleges, and churches. This was the first chance for cotton pickers and college students to see and hear an African American poet. They no more expected an African American to be a poet than to be president. Until his death in 1967, Hughes read to, talked with, and encouraged young African Americans. His work opened their eyes to a new universe.

Hughes's travels would take him across this country and around the world. He wrote articles, poems, and stories based on his wanderings. He founded a theater in Harlem and wrote plays for it. He wrote a movie script, his autobiography, and stories about Jesse B. Semple, a Harlem character he had met in a bar. So universal was their vision of human strengths and weaknesses that these books were translated into many languages.

Hughes often worked with composers, writing the story and lyrics for operas, musical folk comedies, and gospel shows. He wrote many books for young readers on black heroes, musicians, jazz, the West Indies, and Africa. He took part in many festivals of music, poetry, and the arts both at home and abroad.

Hughes's life sounds as though it was great fun, and in truth it was. But it was also a life of hardship and many disappointments. Throughout it, he suffered from the discrimination and segregation so common among African Americans and was hounded because of his political views. None of his writings earned him great financial reward, but he lived generously, devoted to helping anyone he could. He had a special gift for friendship as well as for the arts.

He died in 1967 at the age of sixty-five. It was a great loss for everyone who knew him and for the millions of people who loved his work.

Stars

BY LANGSTON HUGHES

O, sweep of stars over Harlem streets,

O, little breath of oblivion that is night.

    A city building

    To a mother's song.

    A city dreaming

    To a lullaby.

Reach up your hand, dark boy, and take a star.

Out of the little breath of oblivion

    That is night,

    Take just

    One star.

Eleanor Roosevelt as Teacher

BY MAUREEN WOLFGARTH

teach because I love it. I cannot give it up." Eleanor Roosevelt spoke these words at a news conference shortly after her husband, Franklin, was elected governor of New York in 1928.

Always fondly remembering Marie Souvestre, her headmistress at Allenswood (the English boarding school that Eleanor attended as a girl), Eleanor found teaching appealing. In 1927, she and two friends, Marion Dickerman and Nancy Cook, bought the Todhunter School in New York City. Todhunter was a fashionable private school for girls in the primary through high school grades.

Eleanor joined the staff as a teacher and vice principal in 1927. She taught the seniors. Her classes included English and American litera-ture, drama, and American history. Her history exams were given in two parts. One part tested a knowledge of facts and dates, while the other asked questions requiring the girls to think for themselves. One of her test questions stated, "Give your reasons for or against allowing women to actively participate in the control of government, politics, and officials through the vote, as well as your reasons for or against women holding office in the government."

A course Eleanor especially enjoyed teaching was called "Happenings," a class on current events. Eleanor wanted the girls to experience things firsthand. Her students visited courts, police lineups, markets, and tenements. She felt it was important for her classes to understand "the

In 1933, the first year of Franklin Roosevelt's presidency, Eleanor and Franklin posed in front of their home in New York City.

connection between the things of the past and things of today."

In making homework assignments, Eleanor used the "project method." She encouraged her students to read, investigate, and visit people and places to complete their projects. Class-book notes such as "look up Vikings," "trace the trade routes better," and "be more exact" show that Eleanor also was receiving an education.

When Franklin became governor, Eleanor continued to teach at Todhunter. On Sunday evening, she left Albany and traveled to New York City by train. She taught from nine to one on Mondays, nine to five on Tuesdays, and nine to eleven on Wednesdays. Late Wednesday afternoon, she returned to the Executive Mansion. She once admitted, "I prepare my lessons on the train going up and down." For a time, she even taught a class for Todhunter graduates and their friends after Franklin was elected president and she moved to Washington, D.C.

During the 1930s, Eleanor contin-ued to be involved with Todhunter. She attended opening day and graduation exercises, held an annual party for the school's staff, and invited each graduating class to the White House for a weekend.

Speaking about Eleanor, Marion Dickerman said, "Teaching gave her some of the happiest moments in her life. She loved it. The girls worshipped her. She was a very inspiring person."

It is evident from all Eleanor's accomplishments that she lived her life following the advice she gave a graduating class from Todhunter: "Don't dry up by inaction but go out and do new things. Learn new things and see new things with your own eyes." She was truly a teacher who believed in what she taught.

Life After the White House

BY RUSSELL ROBERTS

W hen a newspaperwoman asked Eleanor Roosevelt for a statement several days after her husband's death, the former first lady simply said, "The story is over."

But for Anna Eleanor Roosevelt, the story was far from over. In the years following Franklin's death in 1945, she became a symbol of hope, caring, and love to people throughout the world. It was no wonder that she was known as the "First Lady of the World."

Eleanor Roosevelt was worried that when she first left the White House, "I might find times when I wouldn't know what to do with myself." But that worry quickly passed in December 1945, when President Harry S. Truman appointed her as a member of the American delegation to the United Nations (UN). Like her husband, Eleanor firmly believed that the UN was the world's best hope for avoiding another war. Although female delegates were very rare at that time, during her seven years as an American delegate, she won the respect and admiration of men and women alike for her courage and honesty.

She considered her "most important task" at the UN to be her role as

> Eleanor Roosevelt considered her "most important task" at the UN to be her role as chairwoman of the Commission on Human Rights.

chairwoman of the Commission on Human Rights. The duty of this commission was to define the basic rights of people all over the world, such as the right to free speech and a fair trial, so that a government could not deny those rights. Trying to get nations with different customs, religions, and governments to agree on these rights was a difficult task, but somehow Eleanor Roosevelt succeeded. The UN General Assembly adopted the Universal Declaration of Human Rights on December 10, 1948.

President Truman admired and respected Eleanor Roosevelt. He called her the "First Lady of the World" and asked her whenever possible to visit foreign countries on behalf of the United States. In turn, Eleanor would regularly write or talk to Truman about issues that she thought were important.

One of the more important matters on which Eleanor Roosevelt advised President Truman was the creation of a Jewish homeland, known as Israel. She knew that the support of the United States was vital if Israel was to become a country, as many other countries were not in favor of establishing a Jewish state. Thanks in part to Eleanor Roosevelt, the United States backed the creation of Israel, which became a nation in 1948.

When President Dwight D. Eisenhower, a Republican, took office in 1953, Eleanor Roosevelt, a Democrat, found her pipeline to the president's office shut off. She remained as busy as ever, however. Her daily newspaper column, called "My Day," enabled her to speak out publicly on important issues. She wrote books and lectured frequently. She opposed Senator Joseph McCarthy's "hunt" for Communists because she saw that people were becoming afraid of speaking freely for fear that they would be labeled as such. As one of the most admired women in the world, Eleanor Roosevelt traveled to many different countries, including Japan, Yugoslavia, the Soviet Union, Israel, and India.

Eleanor also became a strong supporter of women's rights. Part of the reason for her trip to Japan in 1952 was because Japanese women were having a difficult time adjusting to their new role in the democratic society that the United States had created for them after World War II. Before then, a Japanese wife was practically a slave in her own household. Eleanor talked to many groups of Japanese women, explaining the theories of democracy and freedom under which they were now living. Always a believer in the equality of women as citizens, her last official position was chairwoman of President John F. Kennedy's Commission on the Status of Women in 1961.

"Misery is the same in any country," Eleanor once told a Japanese farmer, and she fought injustice at home just as hard as she did in other countries. She was instrumental in getting the Democrats to favor desegregation for blacks during the 1956 election, even though it angered many of the party's southern supporters. From 1960 on, she was constantly in touch with Attorney General Robert F. Kennedy about civil rights for blacks living in the South.

Although Eleanor maintained an apartment in New York City, she felt most at home at her Hyde Park estate, where her large family would gather for holiday celebrations. Eleanor's relationships with her own children were sometimes trying, but her grandchildren made her very happy. They wanted to learn from her many experiences. Her grandson Franklin says that she

was the most important influence in his life.

Children held a special place in Eleanor's heart. "I am interested in every child who needs help, and I am ready to help him," she said. She enjoyed talking to children, and they to her; she always spoke to them as one friend to another. She also actively supported many different organizations that helped children, such as the Wiltwyck School and the Jewish group called Youth Aliyah.

Eleanor Roosevelt's door was always open, no matter whether a person was a president or a pauper. She attended political affairs, wrote her daily column, and tried to help people right up until November 7, 1962, when she died at her New York City apartment at age seventy-eight. At her funeral, which was attended by dignitaries from all over the world, UN Ambassador (and good friend) Adlai Stevenson said, "What other single human being has touched and transformed the existence of so many?"

AN INTERVIEW WITH
Shirley Chisholm
FEBRUARY 1983

Editor's Note: Shirley Chisholm became the first black woman ever elected to the United States Congress in 1968. From January 1969 to January 1983, she served as a representative from Brooklyn, New York. Chisholm was born in Brooklyn in 1924. She graduated from Columbia University in New York City and worked as a teacher and as the director of a day nursery before entering politics in 1964. Her first elective office was as a member of the New York State Assembly. In 1972, Chisholm campaigned to be the Democratic party nominee for president. Although she did not win, she wrote a book, *The Good Fight,* which tells the story of her campaign. She has also written an autobiography, *Unbought and Unbossed.* Chisholm chose not to run for reelection in 1982.

When you were a child, did you feel that you might someday want to be involved in politics and government?

No, although when I was a young girl, my grandmother told me many times that I was special and that I was going to accomplish many things in my life. I know that my early formative years under my grandmother's strict guidance gave me the discipline and confidence I have relied on to get where I am today.

What role has your religious background played in your work in Congress?

I grew up in a Quaker brethren

home. My strong faith in God and the religious ideals I learned as a girl have been a great help to me, especially when I have been misunderstood and unfairly criticized.

Why did you decide to run for Congress? Were you worried by the fact that no black woman had ever been elected?

When I decided to run for the U.S. House of Representatives in 1968, I was convinced that I had the ability and experience needed to represent the people of that district. Apparently, the people agreed, and I was elected. The fact that no other black woman had served in the Congress did not worry me at all because I knew I could do the job as well as anyone else.

What did you hope to accomplish for the people you represented, and how did your goals change through the years?

I promised my constituents that I would fight for peace and for equal opportunity in education and employment. Because of the increasing threat of war today, and because we have not yet achieved full equality for women and minorities in this country, these are still my major goals.

How were you treated by your colleagues in Congress during those early days? Did the treatment surprise you?

When I first came to Congress, I was treated as a kind of curio,* but this did not really surprise me. Everyone wanted to get a good look at me, and they waited to see if I was going to calm down and be a quiet team player. After a few months, they got used to my presence, but I think that many of them never got used to my outspokenness or insistence on always doing what I knew to be the right thing to do.

Did you feel any special pressure because of being a black woman in Congress? If so, how did you overcome this?

I felt a double pressure. As a black and as a woman, I have heard constant appeals from Americans of both these groups who look to me for leadership, and I have faced discriminatory attitudes by others who have had trouble accepting the fact that someone other than a white male can be intelligent and effective in our society.

* *
*A curio is an interesting or unusual object — something that makes people curious.

Shirley Chisholm

What did you hope to accomplish by running for president in 1972?

In 1972, I felt that there were extremely important national issues that had to be debated, and I made sure they were. I also hoped to provide encouragement by example for other minorities and women to become active participants in our political system.

What are some of the biggest changes in America you've seen during your time in office, and how do you feel about them?

Thousands of women and blacks have entered the mainstream of economic and political life in the past decade. This is a great accomplishment for those individuals and for our nation. The clear challenge is to continue that trend over the coming years.

More Famous People

Following are a few of the many other famous New Yorkers.

Edith Wharton

etween the nineteenth and twentieth centuries, New York City's "high society" lived in elegance and luxury. **Mrs. William Astor** (born Caroline Schermerhorn) set the rules for society life among the aristocratic group called "the four hundred." The famous author **Edith Wharton,** who was born into New York's "high society," wrote about this group in her novels *The House of Mirth* and *The Age of Innocence.*

New York has had its share of colorful mayors. **James John Walker,** known as "Gentleman Jimmy" for his good looks and fashionable clothes, was mayor from 1926 to 1932. He was forced to resign in 1932 due to a political scandal.

Ed Koch was the colorful mayor of New York City from 1977 to 1989. Born and educated in the city, he described himself as mayor of a city "that has more Jews than live in Jerusalem, more Italians than live in Rome, more Irish than live in Dublin, more blacks than live in Nairobi and more Puerto Ricans than live in San Juan." "And," added Koch, "...we have learned to live with each other."

HOW TO TAKE PICTURES

BY GENE H. RUSSELL

New Yorkers, famous and just regular people, have an impact on the city every day.
You probably know someone who is making a difference for others. Write your own article
about a New Yorker and take his or her photograph or draw a picture to go with it.

If you do not own a camera, getting started in photography is still within your reach. Many schools and libraries have cameras you can borrow, and photography clubs sponsor exhibits and offer classes. There is a photographer's paradise out there waiting, so let us begin taking pictures.

Focusing. Nonadjustable cameras have a fixed position lens and require no adjustment in taking pictures. Other simple cameras may have three lens positions for taking close-up, middle-distance, and distant pictures.

Adjustable camera lenses vary greatly. A common adjustable focusing lens will produce sharp images from about 0.6 meters (2 feet) to infinity (everything beyond 50 feet). Most adjustable cameras have built-in focusing aids on their viewing screens that are extremely helpful in bringing an image into sharp focus. On some models, the widest outside ring on the lens is turned to focus these cameras.

Shutter. Simple cameras may have only a single shutter speed. Others may have two, three, or more speed settings, identified by weather symbols. A fast shutter speed is needed for bright conditions, while a slow or medium-slow shutter speed is appropriate for overcast days. Adjustable cameras have a variety of shutter speed settings, ranging from 1 second to 1/1000 second. When hand-holding one of these cameras, set the shutter speed dial for 1/60 second or faster to eliminate camera movement while taking the picture. The speed of the shutter controls the recording of subject movement on the film and also the length of time that light is allowed to hit or expose the film.

Aperture. Once again, simple cameras may use weather symbols for different-size openings of the aperture. In most cameras, the size of the aperture is indicated by its f number. The lower the f number, the larger the opening that admits light to the film. The aperture setting is also a factor in image sharpness. The aperture controls a zone of sharpness, known as depth of field, on either side of the focused subject. Pictures taken with a high f number will have a larger area of sharpness than those snapped with a lower f number. Keep the camera set for the higher f numbers (small aperture openings) if you like pictures with sharp images.

Exposure. When taking a picture, hold the camera level and gently squeeze or press the shutter button. Make sure the camera case, strap, and your fingers are away from the front of the lens to avoid being recorded on the film. Steady yourself if the wind is blowing or if the ground is uneven. A telephone pole, a table, or a wall can be used to hold a camera steady. Avoid aiming the camera toward the sun.

This is dangerous to your eyes, plus these pictures rarely turn out. Experiment by taking pictures at various times of day and under a variety of lighting conditions. A flash unit is needed for indoor pictures under artificial lighting and as fill-in lighting in some outdoor situations.

Composition. Be selective of your subject matter and wait for just the right moment to snap the picture. Avoid taking pictures that will have cluttered backgrounds. Whenever you can, get as close as possible to your subject. Place people in your scenic photographs to add perspective and show size comparisons. When using color film, look for bright and colorful subjects to photograph.

Follow-up. After you take a picture, advance the film to the next frame. Unload the film after the last exposure and have it processed promptly. Return the camera to its storage area until your next picture-taking session. When your pictures are processed, examine them closely. There is a skill to taking good pictures, and it can be acquired with patience and practice.

BOOKS TO READ

Theodore Roosevelt Takes Charge *by Nancy Whitelaw* (Morton Grove, Illinois: Albert Whitman & Company, 1992) tells the story of Roosevelt's life, from his childhood and early adulthood to his final battles, and has more than eighty photographs. Particularly handy is a chronology of Roosevelt's life. Grades 4 to 9.

Free to Dream *by Audrey Osofsky* (New York: Lothrop, Lee & Shepard, 1996) presents a portrait of Langston Hughes, from his childhood to his years as a celebrated writer. Grades 4 to 9. Also look for a new edition of Hughes's poems for children, *The Dream Keeper.*

Eleanor Roosevelt *by Caroline Lazo* (Parsippany, New Jersey: Silver Burdett Press, 1993) tells the life story of the First Lady, who was a passionate fighter for human rights. Black-and-white photographs illustrate throughout. Grade 4 and up.

MORE MEDIA

Theodore Roosevelt: Rough Rider to Rushmore (A&E, 1995). In this fifty-minute video, learn how a child who was often ill grew up to be a vigorous president and how a war hero became the nation's first Nobel Peace Prize winner. Contact Theodore Roosevelt Birthplace: (212) 260-1616.

Walt Whitman: An American Dream. This 16-minute video includes information about the poet's life and excerpts of his poetry. It is available through the Walt Whitman Birthplace State Historic Site, his 1819 home on Long Island, now a museum. Contact Walt Whitman Birthplace: (516) 427-5240.

PLACES TO VISIT

Hamilton Grange National Memorial. The home of Alexander and Betsy Hamilton contains some of the Hamiltons' furniture and other possessions. Guided tours and a slide show will help you learn more about Alexander Hamilton's public and private lives, his family, and the history of the building.

Theodore Roosevelt Birthplace National Historic Site. Roosevelt was born here in October 1858. The reconstructed brownstone includes rooms with furniture from his time and exhibits about his life.

Studio Museum in Harlem. This small art museum includes historic photographs of Harlem by James Van DerZee.

The City That Means Business

ASK MOST PEOPLE WHAT THEY THINK OF WHEN THEY HEAR THE NAME "New York City," and they may say skyscrapers. Sometimes people say Wall Street or Broadway. These are all part of the business of the city. Millions of people make their living here, and the work they do affects businesses in countries around the world.

The skyscrapers of Wall Street are the home of the New York Stock Exchange. This is the market where stocks are bought and sold. A stock is a share of ownership in a corporation. The money from stocks helps companies to buy the goods or equipment they need to grow. Wall Street has been a center of business since our country began. Even then, you could see well-dressed people rushing to work.

Would you believe that the stock exchange started under a tree on Wall Street? Attend the meeting on May 17,

1792, when twenty-four men started an organization that eventually became known as the New York Stock Exchange.

If all this sounds confusing, do not worry. You will meet Jeffrey Little, who worked on Wall Street and will explain how the stock market works.

New York is famous for its ticker tape parades. The Yankees had a ticker tape parade when they won the World Series in 1996. But what is ticker tape? You will find out the answer to that mystery and why there are no more "real" ticker tape parades.

Sometimes businesses have treated workers badly. In the early 1900s, many poor immigrants worked in sweatshops. These were factories with unhealthy and unsafe conditions. One day a terrible fire broke out in a New York sweatshop, killing 146 people. Discover how this tragedy led to the start of a union to bring about improved working conditions.

Meet a New York City firefighter and find out about the many different kinds of jobs people do here every day. Then take part in a labor game called "Welcome to the Working World!" on pages 186–187.

Taking Stock of Wall Street

· ·

Less than a mile long, Wall Street crosses the tip of Manhattan Island, a small street in one of the largest cities in the world. It is one of several narrow, twisting city streets that three hundred years ago were cow paths and dusty lanes in the tiny settlement that was the beginning of New York City. But when someone says "Wall Street," most people do not think of a tar and concrete roadway lined with tall office buildings. They think of the stock exchange and investment banks, stocks and bonds, and investing money to make more money. It is a little street, but its name brings to mind high finance and the excitement of the stock market.

It was not just by chance that a small street on the tip of an island grew to become one of the leading financial centers of the world. The Upper Bay at the mouth of the Hudson River is the best natural harbor on the east coast of North America. It was an ideal location for settlers to build and trade to flourish.

The city that grew there and the street itself were the site of many key events in American history. New York was one of the most important cities in Colonial America, a busy center of trade and commerce. It was home to many Revolutionary leaders, who often met to discuss their ideas as well as their business in the taverns around Wall Street. The United States' first president was inaugurated on the street, as the city became the nation's capital after the Revolutionary War.

But even when the government moved away, business remained. Because New York's thriving trade made a lot of money available for investment, the city was considered the best market for federal bonds sold to finance the country's war debt. Along with those bonds, brokers also began to sell stocks, small shares of ownership issued by banks and fire insurance companies to raise capital (money for development). Called a securities market, this business grew rapidly in New York, and most of it took place on or near Wall Street.

Today Wall Street is the name given to the marketplace for the investment bankers, brokers, securities analysts, underwriters, and customers involved in stock trading. Their activities are part of the economic process that helps to create new companies and jobs nationwide. Over time, the street gave the stock market its name, and the stock market gave the street its fame.

Beneath the Buttonwood Tree

BY KAREN E. HONG

Most days, more than three hundred million shares of stock are traded on the New York Stock Exchange. The value of an individual share may change only a little, but because of the volume of business, what happens each day on the exchange affects the world.

Like investors today, some early Americans committed their money to ventures they thought would earn a profit. Some bought and sold commodities such as molasses, tobacco, and furs. Others speculated in land or insured cargoes against loss at sea.

With the establishment of banks, shares of stock became available to the public. The first U.S. Congress, meeting in Federal Hall on Wall Street in 1789, authorized the issue of eighty million dollars in government bonds to pay the Revolutionary War debt. Now there were securities, stocks, and government bonds to be bought and sold but no organized way of conducting that business.

If an investor was interested in trading a stock, he might advertise in the newspapers or pass word of his interest along in the Wall Street coffeehouses. As trading activity increased in the winter of 1791–1792, Wall Street businessmen began to schedule auctions for the sale of stocks and bonds just as they had in the past for commodities.

Soon merchants were holding daily securities auctions at 22 Wall Street. The auctioneer received a commission for each stock and bond sold,

as did each buyer's agent, or broker. Buyers actively competed for the stock or bond, with its sale going to the high-est bidder, while sellers simply offered their shares for the highest price. Some businessmen came to the auction only to note current prices. After the auction, these men offered the same securities for sale with a lower commission rate.

On May 17, 1792, twenty-four men met beneath the buttonwood tree facing 68 Wall Street. Representing twenty-one individuals and three two-man partnerships, the men signed a document now known as the Buttonwood Agreement. They agreed to trade securities only with each other, to charge a fixed commission rate, and to avoid other auctions. In forming this simple agreement, these men established an organization that would one day be known as the New York Stock Exchange.

For a while the buttonwood brokers continued to meet and conduct their business under the buttonwood tree. The group moved indoors to the Tontine Coffee House at Wall and Water streets when it was completed in 1793.

By 1817, the security business was thriving. The U.S. government had issued bonds to help finance the War of 1812, and the peace of 1814 brought prosperity as New York emerged as the major American port.

On March 8, 1817, the buttonwood brokers adopted a constitution creating the New York Stock and Exchange Board. More formal than their earlier agreement, the constitution set down rules for membership, the conduct of sales, commission rates, and the delivery of contracts. Every morning, the seated members listened to the list of securities to be auctioned and made bids and offers as each was called out. Today, although members no longer sit, they are said to have seats on the New York Stock Exchange.

Through the years, the New York Stock Exchange has modified the way it does business to keep up with the growth of the stock market. Continuous trading replaced the calls of stocks that had taken place at set times. Only two years after their successful testing, telephones were installed, linking brokers on the trading floor with their offices. Although the New York Stock Exchange has moved many times since 1792, it has stayed on or near Wall Street, close to the buttonwood tree.

How Wall Street Works

AN INTERVIEW WITH JEFFREY LITTLE, APRIL 1990

BY HARRY GARDINER

Although Wall Street is one of the best-known streets in the United States, what goes on there remains a mystery to most people. One man who knows what goes on and can clearly explain it is Jeffrey Little, who began his Wall Street career in the early 1960s. A finance graduate of New York University, he has worked as an accountant for a retail brokerage firm, as an instructor of technical analysis in a brokerage trading center, as a securities analyst, and as a stock portfolio manager and advisory committee member for a major mutual fund. He also has written several books about Wall Street.

What is Wall Street?

It is one of the major financial centers of the world — a marketplace where stocks and bonds are bought and sold.

Can the stock market be explained in an easily understandable way?

Yes. People become part owners or shareholders of corporations by buying stocks and contributing money to set the wheels in motion for building an ongoing enterprise that later employs people with the major purpose of making a profit. We need to get away from the idea that profit is bad. If a company is successful and makes a profit, part of this money can be put back into the company to build more factories and put more people to work. It is the investment process and the incentive to develop new products that help to raise our standard of living.

The floor of the New York Stock Exchange is always a hectic place.

How did you first become interested in the stock market?

My grandmother got me interested. When I was twelve, I bought two shares of General Motors with some money I had saved over the summer. The stock price went up. I was really excited and thought, "Where's this been all my life?" During lunchtime at school, I would run across the street to one of the brokerage firms nearby to watch the ticker tape (see pages

175–176) and see the prices of stocks marked up on the chalkboard. I'd listen to the cheers as a million shares were traded on some days. In high school, I decided I wanted to work on Wall Street. I later went to New York University and majored in finance.

How can students learn more about the stock market?

Probably the best way is to get schools to explain more about the stock market. There used to be programs in schools in which local businessmen helped students design a product, form a company, sell stock in that company, make the product, and sell it in the community. It was a great learning experience. Teachers could have pupils select some stocks from the newspaper, pretend to buy and sell them, and follow their progress in the financial pages. Some of this is being done today, but the subject deserves much more attention than it's getting.

How has the stock market changed during the past few years?

It is more confusing today than it has ever been because there are so many intertwined factors. For example, today there is a global market, which includes the stock exchanges in New York, Tokyo, London, and other cities. There is a much greater dependence on currency rates, exchange rates, index options, programmed trading, and leveraged buy outs. These can be complicated and were not as significant in the simpler days of the 1950s.

Do you have any final thoughts?

When I first got interested in the stock market, there was an expression "Own your share of American business." That really says it all. When you buy a share of stock, you should think of being a part of the process, being a part owner of the company, and sharing in the benefits through dividends, rather than simply trading a piece of paper because you think you'll be able to sell it at a higher price. If you think of it in those terms, you have a greater respect for the system and what it's all about.

The Mystery of the Ticker

BY SHARI LYN ZUBER

Members of the stock exchange in the early 1900s examine recent sales on ticker tape near their telephones at the side of the trading floor.

Before the invention of the ticker, brokers in offices away from the stock exchange floor had no way of knowing the most recent price that a particular stock was selling for. The stock exchange was a crowded, chaotic place, with brokers and clerks jamming the hall trying to learn the latest prices in the trading room. Prices were jotted down on a pad of paper, and messengers, known as pad shovers, rushed them back to the brokers' offices so customers could have the latest information to make decisions about buying and selling.

For brokers outside of New York City, no immediate communication was available until after 1844, when Samuel Morse proved that long-distance telegraphy was possible. Stock prices could be sent over the telegraph, but doing so was slow. The telegraph could send only fifteen to thirty words per minute, and having to decode the Morse code took even more time.

In 1867, Boston inventor E.A. Calahan, who had worked with the American Telegraph Company for years, came up with the idea of a telegraphic instrument that could print stock figures. He spent several months perfecting his printer, which was called the stock ticker because of the sound it

made. The machine was a printing telegraph with a moving type wheel that wrote stock and gold quotations on a moving paper tape. Calahan and others formed the Gold & Stock Telegraph Company to make the ticker and sell its services to Wall Street brokers.

By the 1880s, after several improvements, stock tickers were transmitting 285 characters per minute. Improvements continued, and by 1930 black metallic box tickers typed out 500 characters per minute, or approximately 85 trades. On December 2, 1964, sleek new "900" tickers were introduced. These could print out 900 characters, or 150 transactions, per minute.

Two years later, a computer system that permitted almost instantaneous transmission of quotations from the floor was introduced. Within a few years, tickers were largely phased out. Today a computer flashes transactions as quickly as you can read them across a large screen above the trading floor, while terminals and screens at each post record the transactions as soon as they take place.

Sweatshops and Unions

BY KAREN E. HONG

The quitting bell rang at 4:45 P.M. to mark the end of the workday at the Triangle Shirtwaist Company. Located on the eighth, ninth, and tenth floors of the Asch Building at the corner of Washington Place and Greene Street in New York City, the company manufactured shirtwaists, flimsy blouses with tight waists and billowy sleeves that were popular in the early 1900s. Girls and women, mostly recent Italian and Russian Jewish immigrants, sat close together, bent over sewing machines and surrounded by piles of cloth on rolls and in scrap baskets.

As the girls began to file out of the crowded eighth-floor workroom, one noticed smoke and flames coming from a rag bin under a table. Her yell alerted others, who threw water from nearby pails on the flames. But a draft sent burning scraps through the room. Flimsy fabric and wooden tables and chairs were ready fuel for the fire.

Screaming, panic-stricken girls tried to escape as the fire spread to the ninth and tenth floors. Some girls rushed the stairways, only to find the doors locked. On the ninth floor, a barrel of sewing machine oil blocked a stairway until the flames ignited it, cutting off the exit. A few knew about and used the fire escape, hidden behind shuttered

> Girls and women, mostly recent Italian and Russian Jewish immigrants, sat close together, bent over sewing machines and surrounded by piles of cloth on rolls and in scrap baskets.

windows. But the intense heat soon joined with the weight of those escaping to twist the slats and railings. Finally, the fire escape collapsed.

Elevators carried workers to safety until the heat bent the tracks on the elevator shaft. New York firemen, using their tallest ladders, were able to reach only the sixth floor. In desperation, girls jumped out of the windows, sometimes in twos and threes, to escape the inferno.

The firemen had the blaze under control within thirty minutes, but for many workers, it was too late. One hundred forty-six Triangle employees, mostly young Jewish women, died that Saturday, March 25, 1911. The disaster shocked and enraged the public and fueled the labor union movement.

Since 1870, Jews from eastern Europe, especially Russia, had come to the United States to escape discrimination and oppression. Many of those who settled in New York City worked in the garment industry as they had in Russia. To survive, an entire family might work long hours for inadequate wages in a dark, airless, unsanitary sweatshop. Workers dared not complain lest they be replaced by the numerous recent immigrants desperate for work.

These conditions led Jews to join the labor union movement. In 1885, the Jewish Workingmen's Union was formed. The United Hebrew Trades was organized in 1888 and became the first permanent federation of Jewish organizations. As strikes proved effective, other branches of the garment industry began to organize. Two largely Jewish labor unions, the International Ladies' Garment Workers' Union (ILGWU) and the Amalgamated Clothing Workers of America, led workers in the clothing industry after 1900.

The tragedy of the Triangle fire exposed how much more needed to be done to protect factory workers. The ILGWU took the lead in pushing for reforms. Wages increased, working hours decreased, and child labor was eliminated. Laws were enacted establishing new sanitary and safety standards. By 1914, workers in the garment industry and elsewhere were better protected against exploitation by factory owners.

FEBRUARY 1990

An Interview With a New York City Firefighter

BY THOMAS R. MILLER

When fire breaks out in a building, the lives and safety of the people inside depend on a swift response by firefighters. These men and women regularly risk their lives to save and protect others. Tom Ahern, a firefighter with Engine Company 47 in New York City, formed KIDSAFE, a program designed to teach children what to do in case of a fire. Here he answers questions about his job and fire safety.

Why did you decide to become a firefighter?

Family ties — my dad was a mechanic for the New York City Fire Department for thirty-seven years. I've always liked the idea of civil service and helping out.

What happens when a fire alarm goes off?

When an alarm goes off, I put on my boots, my helmet, my turnout coat — I think the name comes from the expression "turn out," to go out — and sit on the fire engine. Then we get out into the street, and I listen to the radio. If there is a fire, I roll up my boots, and we pull up in front of the burning building. If I'm the first one to go in, I stretch out the hose line. I go to the back of the fire engine, pick up the hose, and get ready to stretch it up to wherever the fire is. Another firefighter opens up the door with an ax. Then I go into the burning building to fight the fire.

How do you put out a fire?

Teamwork is the way to put it out. Four firefighters work in the fire engine with one driver, called a chauffeur. When they pull up to the fire, they each have a specific responsibility. The first two firefighters are on the hose line. They take the hose off and go to the seat of the fire — the apartment door or wherever the fire is. The third and fourth "flake it out" — that is, they help stretch the hose line so there are no kinks. The chauffeur hooks up to the hydrant.

The water comes from the hydrant through a suction hose onto the fire engine, then goes into the pumps, which build up the pressure. Then it gets pumped out into the hose, which is already flaked out up into the building. The chauffeur can change the pressure so that more water can come through if needed.

There's teamwork between two different companies as well: the engine company, which I belong to, and the truck company, which evacuates people with the aerial ladder or the tower ladder and gets people off their fire escapes. The truck company is more involved with rescuing people and ventilation: breaking windows and opening holes in roofs so that the smoke can get out of the house.

How many firefighters are needed to fight a typical fire?

A one-alarm fire would get a normal response: three fire engines, two trucks, and one battalion chief. A four-alarm fire would have one hundred to two hundred firefighters. That's a big fire. We've had ten alarms, but that's very unusual.

Are there any special problems fighting fires in New York City?

There are all different types of structures here. We have skyscrapers and brownstones and university buildings, row frames [a row of houses sharing a single frame] and wooden houses. Because of the different types of buildings, we fight fires in different ways. We may fight a brownstone fire in a certain way because it might have several entrances and floors. A row frame might have a common attic called a cockloft [a small space below the ridge of the roof], and a cockloft fire can spread down the entire row of homes.

New York City firefighters bring people out of the upper stories of a smoky building.

How has firefighting changed over the years?

A hundred years ago, fire departments had horses. Then came fire engines and different pumps as technology improved. In the early days, firefighters didn't have masks; they had to take the heat and smoke. They would stretch up their turnout coats to get a couple of breaths away from the smoke. Today we have a breathing apparatus designed by NASA that gives us fifteen or twenty minutes of air and gives us a signal when it's running out of air so we can get out of the burning building.

What should a person do if he or she is in a fire?

If you're in a burning building, the most important thing is to get out. The basic survival tip is *stay low while you go*. Where does smoke go? Smoke goes up. Where do we go if smoke goes up? We go down. Those levels are like night and day. Don't jump out of your bed; roll off your bed. When you're on the floor, you should stay low while you go, which is a smoke crawl. The reason why staying low is so important is that you can often breathe an inch or two or even three inches above the ground. There's a good chance you'll find breathable air at the level where your nose is when you're crawling. But if you stand up, you might be overcome by smoke. That's the message that millions of people have to learn: Stay low while you go. If your clothes catch on fire, that's when you stop, drop, and roll.

How do fires get started?

Usually by accident: smoking in bed, children playing with matches, ovens or electrical appliances left on. Fire marshals investigate immediately after a fire and try to find out where it began. They're trained to detect how fires are set. Sometimes they can tell that something was deliberately burned by the smell of the smoke and by the way the smoke looks.

How can we prevent fires?

You can prevent fires by trying to keep your house clear of the possibility of a fire starting. Make sure the curtains aren't right over the stove. Don't put newspapers on heaters or radiators. If there are lighters or matches around, give them to your parents. Everybody should have smoke detectors, especially in the kitchen. I think that's very important, because if a fire starts, you want to be awake and know about it. Smoke detectors will give you a signal that a fire has started.

What do firefighters do when they're not out fighting fires?

New York City has the busiest fire department in the world. We're ready at all times. The firefighters live in the firehouse. We have committee work: making the beds, cleaning the bathrooms, and mopping the floors. We go out and inspect buildings to make sure that they have proper fire escapes, exit signs, and no obstructions in the hallways. We respond to a lot of emergencies. We rescue people with heart attacks, people with breathing problems, people in car accidents, people who fall in manholes. We'll put up a ladder and go up in a tree to get somebody's cat. We'll help out in most situations.

Looking for a Job?

BY DIANA CHILDRESS

I t's a nice place to visit," some people say about New York City, "but I wouldn't want to live there." Well, how about working there? More than three and a half million people do. What kinds of jobs do they have, and where do they do them?

One-fifth of New York's workers commute into the city from neighboring New Jersey, northern New York, or Long Island, while almost half live in one borough of the city and work in another. Many of the rest travel within their boroughs. That means that New York needs a large number of transit workers to run the buses, taxis, subways, railroads, and ferries that get people to their jobs. The subways alone carry more than a billion passengers a year.

If you're looking for a job, why not try New York? Chances are the Big Apple has an exciting one for you.

Where do all these riders go? Many head downtown to the Financial District, at the southernmost tip of Manhattan — that is, Wall Street. Here many tall buildings are crowded together on the narrow, twisting lanes of the original Colonial settlement. Stacked above the dark and windy canyons formed by these skyscrapers are the offices of bankers, insurance brokers, corporation lawyers, stock analysts and traders — "the largest concentration of business expertise in the world," city planners brag.

Two centuries ago, brokers first met here under a buttonwood tree to buy and sell shares for companies in need of capital (see pages 169–171). At that time, shipping on the nearby East

River dominated the business scene. New York soon became the busiest harbor in the Americas. The need for more horizontal space to load and unload containers later drove shipping away from the crowded waterfront of Manhattan to Brooklyn, New Jersey, and Staten Island, but the financial institutions that developed from shipping expanded and prospered.

New York grew into a major manufacturing center after the Civil War, but many factories have left the city for more elbow-room or lower-paid workers elsewhere. One industry that remains is the garment industry, popularly known as the "rag trade."

New Yorkers have manufactured clothing since the earliest days, when sailors needed cheap, durable garments. Although reduced in size from its peak in the 1940s, the garment industry employs more workers than any other private enterprise. It even has its own section of town: Part of midtown Manhattan is officially named the Fashion Center.

If you go up Seventh Avenue north of Thirty-fourth Street on any business day, you will probably be dodging dresses being wheeled on racks through traffic. About 175,000 people work in this twenty-five-block area — designers, manufacturers, models, wholesalers, and retailers of clothing, textiles, accessories, trimmings, and furs.

North, south, and east of the Fashion Center, the communications trades thrive. Editors and designers oversee the publication of thousands of books and magazines, generating almost half of the nationwide earnings of those two industries. Television executives, camera operators, announcers, and reporters from the three leading television networks and several cable networks also have their offices and studios in midtown Manhattan. Close by, mostly along Madison Avenue, copywriters and art directors at more than a thousand advertising agencies hatch ideas and plan campaigns for selling products the world over. Many accountants and lawyers provide financial services and legal advice for all these businesses.

Of course, not all employees in New York work in offices from nine to five. In the Theater District, which straddles Broadway north of Forty-second Street, and at Lincoln Center and Carnegie Hall farther uptown, actors, directors, stage managers, set and lighting designers, dancers, singers, and musicians put on shows and concerts every night. Late-hour jobs also exist in Greenwich Village and SoHo, between midtown and downtown, where many artists, writers, and musicians live and work. Galleries, jazz clubs, "off-Broadway" theaters, small cafés, craft shops, and bookstores dot these neighborhoods. The businesses are often staffed by part-time workers waiting for a big break that will make them full-time actors. The glamour of New York attracts visitors from every country. Tourism provides income for tour guides, hotel and restaurant owners, housekeepers, chefs, bartenders, and waiters — and for horse-and-buggy drivers in Central Park.

New York City is not just the "Mecca of the dollar," as one cynical tourist put it. Teachers and researchers, professors and scientists, librarians and museum curators also play important roles in the intellectual life of the city. They, too, have their "districts," whether campuses, such as New York University and Columbia University, the "Museum Mile" on upper Fifth Avenue, the research libraries in midtown, or the clusters of hospitals along First Avenue.

Transportation, finance, the garment industry, publishing, the mass media, advertising, the arts, tourism, universities, libraries, and museums — these are only some of New York's major employers. You can do almost anything in a city this large. How would you like to work in "high steel," specializing in riveting the beams of future skyscrapers? Or interpret diplomats' speeches at the United Nations? Or police the evening crowds in Times Square from atop a horse? If you're looking for a job, why not try New York? Chances are the Big Apple has an exciting one for you.

Start Here:

You have applied for membership in the union. Now you're waiting for the paperwork to come through. When you roll a **6** or a **1**, you're in. Move ahead one space.

You like your job, and being in the union gives you a sense of security. The pay isn't great, but the hours are reasonable. Next roll:

3, 4, 5, or 6: You are a natural at Rollerblade assembly. Move ahead five spaces.

1 or 2: You have a few things to learn. Stay put for one turn. On next turn, don't roll, just move ahead five spaces.

Don't roll! Just when you thought you were sunk, you inherit some money from your Great-Aunt Henrietta. Move ahead five spaces.

Alas! You have to get a weekend job to make ends meet. Roll a **4** and move ahead that many spaces, or move back one space.

WELCOME TO THE

★ **ACTIVITY** ★

BY SAM DUSTIN

You have just gotten a job at the local Rollerblade factory, working on the assembly line. Your fellow workers encourage you to join the union, so you sign up.

Experience the ups and downs of factory work when you play this game with one or more of your friends or family. All you need is one die and a playing piece for each player. At the beginning of each turn, read the directions on the space you're on. Roll the die only once per turn (unless the directions say "Don't roll"). Have fun!

Hurray! Management and the union agree on a negotiated contract. Laid-off workers are hired back. Wages are set at a reasonable level to ride out the recession. Management settles for lower profits until the economy recovers. When you roll a **6**, move ahead one space.

You are the "Rollerblade Assembler of the Year" and get to carry the union banner in the Labor Day parade. Have a nice holiday!

Next roll:

5 or 6: Management comes to the realization that it needs the union assemblers back. Move ahead one space.

1, 2, 3, or 4: While participating in the strike, you come down with a nasty case of Picketer's Flu. Go straight home and get into bed. Move back one space.

Picketer's Flu has you in its grip. Next roll:

4, 5, or 6: You followed the doctor's advice and are now ready to go back to the factory. Move ahead two spaces.

1, 2, or 3: You are staying up late and eating junk food. You'll never get rid of the flu that way! Get back in bed and stay there until you roll high (**4, 5, or 6**).

Next roll:

4, 5, or 6: Management is wearing down. Move ahead three spaces.

1, 2, or 3: Management calls in scabs to replace striking workers. But scabs are not as skilled at Rollerblade assembly, and management knows it. Move ahead two spaces.

Strike! All members of the union picket the factory. Production comes to a screeching halt. Next roll:

5 or 6: Management is worried. The strike is working. It looks as if negotiations are in store. Move ahead four spaces.

1, 2, 3, or 4: Management won't budge. Move ahead one space while considering your next move.

Economy collapses! The country is headed for a depression. The demand for Rollerblades is falling rapidly. Big layoffs are predicted. Next roll:

5 or 6: Whew! You're not laid off, but your pay is cut and you have to work more hours. Move ahead one space.

1, 2, 3, or 4: Sorry! You've been laid off until the economy picks up. Move back one space.

You're surprised. How could they lay off a terrific assembler like you? Roll a **2** and move ahead that many spaces, or move back one space.

You have to borrow money from your mom and dad. (How embarrassing!) Roll a **3** and move ahead that many spaces, or move back one space.

Forget that trip to Bermuda. A long weekend at your brother's might be more within your budget. Roll a **2** and move ahead that many spaces, or move back one space.

Oh, no! The cost of living has just gone up (along with the cost of Rollerblades), but your salary hasn't! Next roll:

5 or 6: You're still able to pay the bills, but just barely. Move ahead one space.

1, 2, 3, or 4: Tsk, tsk. You didn't put any savings away for times like these. Move back one space.

The union approaches management about pay increases. Next roll:

3, 4, 5, or 6: Rollerblades are still selling well. Management is willing to negotiate wages. Move ahead two spaces.

1 or 2: Rollerblade sales are in a downward slide. Management is cautious about raising salaries. Stay put for one turn. On next turn, don't roll, just move ahead one space.

WORKING WORLD!

Money is very tight. You have to sell your sports car. Next roll:

4, 5, or 6: You got a good price for the car, and pay-raise negotiations have begun at the factory. Move ahead one space.

1, 2, or 3: You're still waiting for a buyer. Stay put until you roll high (**4, 5, or 6**).

Negotiations end. The union and management agree on a new contract. Next roll:

4, 5, or 6: Congratulations! You got a big raise. Move ahead three spaces.

1, 2, or 3: You didn't get the big raise you wanted, only a small cost-of-living increase. Move ahead one space.

Don't roll! There was a clerical error; you do get the raise after all. Move ahead two spaces.

The heat wave is unbearable, and so are the working conditions. Continue to suffer until you roll a **6** or a **1.** Finally you're getting some sense. You sign your name to the union grievance petition. Move ahead two spaces.

You're getting downright nervous, being out of work so long. When is this recession going to end? Roll a **3** and move ahead that many spaces, or move back one space.

Don't roll! The union has decided to call a strike. You are to report to the picket line right away. Move ahead four spaces.

Next roll:

3, 4, 5, or 6: The grievance procedure worked wonders! Brand-new air conditioners were installed today. Move ahead four spaces.

1 or 2: Management responds favorably to the grievance, but new air conditioners will take a week to arrive. Stay put one turn, then move ahead four spaces.

A heat wave rolls in, and none of the air conditioners are working. Next roll:

4, 5, or 6: You waste no time talking to the union representatives about filing a grievance with management over poor working conditions. Move ahead one space.

1, 2, or 3: Instead of calling upon the union to solve the dilemma, you suffer and feel sorry for yourself. Move back one space.

BOOKS TO READ

You and the Investment World (NYSE Educational Products, 1997) is a publication of the New York Stock Exchange that helps students understand how the stock market works and presents a history of the New York Stock Exchange. Grades 4 to 12.

Great American Businesswomen *by Laura S. Jeffrey* (Springfield, New Jersey: Enslow Publishers, 1996), a group biography, includes the stories of successful businesswomen of the twentieth century. Grade 4 and up.

We Shall Not Be Moved: The Women's Factory Strike of 1909 *by Joan Dash* (New York: Scholastic, 1996) paints a vivid picture of the lives of working-class women in the early 1900s as it relates the conditions leading up to the shirtwaist industry strike, the story of the strike, and its results. Grades 3 to 8.

MORE MEDIA

Understanding the Stock Market (1990). A filmstrip, audiocassette, and guide explain the workings of corporations, stock markets, and stock exchanges. For those who are seeking a challenge. Contact Knowledge Unlimited: (608) 836-6660.

Stock Market Game Web Page. Learn about the stock market through participation! At this Internet site, students receive an imaginary one hundred thousand dollars to invest over a ten-week period. Participants select investments and see how they perform over time. Contact: www.smg2000.org.

PLACES TO VISIT

New York Stock Exchange. The visitors center is open to the public through limited free tickets that are distributed at the 20 Broad Street entrance beginning at 9 A.M. each business day. A tour includes exhibits on how and why the market works, hands-on experience with computer terminals, and a view of the trading floor from the visitors gallery.

American Museum of Financial History. This one-room museum on the site of Alexander Hamilton's law office includes an old ticker tape machine and old seats from the trading posts of the New York Stock Exchange. Changing exhibits focus on various topics in the history of money in the United States.

New York City Fire Museum. This museum displays historic and modern firefighting equipment, including fire engines (hand-pulled, horse-drawn, and motorized), sliding poles, and uniforms from three hundred years of New York City history. Interactive fire safety tours can also be arranged.

The Entertainment Capital of the World

THE CIRCUS, THE THEATER, TELEVISION, MUSIC, DANCE. NAME A form of entertainment, and it can be found in New York City. This is where performers from all over the world come to break into show business. The words to a song about New York say what many performers believe: "If I can make it here, I'll make it anywhere."

Phineas T. Barnum, sometimes called "the greatest showman who ever lived," came to New York in 1834 at the age of twenty-four to seek his fortune. Meet Barnum and find out how he teamed up with another showman to create the Barnum & Bailey Circus. Later renamed the Ringling Bros. and Barnum & Bailey Circus, it is still one of the world's most popular circuses.

In 1939, most people had never heard of television. Radio was the main source of news and entertainment in homes across the country. But that year, New Yorkers got a look at the future. Take a tour of the 1939–1940 New York World's Fair to see some of the eighteen hundred exhibits. The theme of the fair was "Building the World of Tomorrow." Discover which of its predictions came true.

You may never have heard of the Harlem Renaissance, but you probably have heard of its performers and writers. A renaissance is a rebirth or rediscovery and is often a time when much artistic activity takes place. In the 1920s, Harlem was the center of an artistic movement made up of African American writers, poets, dancers, singers, actors, composers, and painters. Come meet people like Bessie Smith, Louis Armstrong, and Duke Ellington. Their work is as popular today as when they first performed it during the Harlem Renaissance.

Did you know that New York City even has a high school devoted to entertainment? Talented students compete to attend La Guardia High School of the Arts, where they can study art, music, dance, or drama. Take a tour of the school and watch an all-student performance.

Of course, children in New York have always made their own entertainment. Check out "City Games" on pages 211–212 to see if you know any of the games played here long ago.

The Greatest Showman Who Ever Lived

BY M.A. CHRISTOPHER

He was called many things — a braggart, an outrageous buffoon, a genius, a fake, and a born liar. He made and lost several fortunes in his lifetime. He was elected mayor of a large city and was a friend of Mark Twain, Abraham Lincoln, and Queen Victoria of England. He was Phineas Taylor Barnum, and some say he was the greatest showman who ever lived.

Phineas Barnum was born in Bethel, Connecticut, on July 5, 1810. Because his father died when he was only fifteen, Phineas had to support the rest of his family. He was a hard worker, and by the time he was twenty-one, he was publisher of a Danbury, Connecticut, weekly newspaper, the *Herald Freedom*. Phineas was an outspoken young man, and it frequently got him into trouble. Several times he was arrested for publishing libel — damaging statements about a person's character — in his paper. Once he spent sixty days in jail. As a result of this incident, he became something of a celebrity in the town.

At the age of twenty-four, Barnum decided to seek his fortune elsewhere. With his wife, Charity, he moved to New York City. There he presented the first of his many exhibits to the public. This was an elderly woman named Joice Heth, who claimed she had been the personal nurse to none other than George Washington. Heth was supposed to be 161 years old, and she had papers to prove it. Many people paid to see and talk with Heth. After her death, her claim was found to be false. Barnum said that he, too, had

THE JOURDAN'S, GREATEST FLYING GYMNASTS OF THE WORLD.
MOST STRIKINGLY NOVEL, DARING AND UNUSUALLY WONDERFUL MID-AIR PERFORMANCES.
THE WORLD'S CHAMPION AND MOST THRILLING AERIAL ARTISTS.

THE WORLD'S GRANDEST, LARGEST, BEST, AMUSEMENT INSTITUTION.

been fooled by the likable old woman.

In 1842, a five-story building in lower Manhattan went up for sale. Barnum bought the thirty-year-old structure and named it Barnum's American Museum. He had his own ideas of what a museum should be, and he filled his with weird displays, sensational exhibits, and all sorts of unusual attractions, as well as ordinary museum exhibits. Although he was not the most educated of men, Barnum was a

This 1891 poster shows one of the many unusual and exciting acts of the Barnum & Bailey Circus.

careful observer of human nature. He knew that people had a natural interest in the unusual and the bizarre. He advertised his museum with posters that said the museum offered "a marvelous assemblage of strangest human beings [and] a wondrous study of nature's wildest vagaries." Barnum roamed the world in search of new and exciting exhibits for his museum and used newspaper ads to tell of his adventures.

P.T. Barnum and his American Museum became an international sensation. The fact that some of his exhibits were proven to be fake never bothered Barnum. He told people that he, too, had been the innocent victim of some dishonest individual. With his warm personality and his clever showmanship, he could overcome any criticism.

One of his more outstanding accomplishments involved Johanna "Jenny" Lind, whom Barnum called the "Swedish Nightingale." Although Lind was already well-known as an opera singer in Europe, she was not known in America. Lind had a wide vocal range, which thrilled her audiences. Barnum took her on a concert tour across the United States, and she became the most popular singer of the time. People flocked to her shows. At an auction for tickets for a Boston performance, one seat sold for $625, a fantastic sum for the day.

Barnum owed his greatest success to a boy named Charles Stratton, a midget who was barely two feet tall. General Tom Thumb, as Barnum renamed Stratton, was taught to sing and dance, and soon he delighted crowds wherever he performed. Barnum took General Tom Thumb on a highly publicized world tour, and the General appeared before the Prince of Wales, King Leopold of Belgium, the viceroy of Egypt, the king of France, and Queen Isabella of Spain.

Then in 1868, fire destroyed the American Museum.

Three years later, P.T. Barnum's Greatest Traveling Museum, Menagerie, Caravan and Hippodrome* was organized. The show's acts included the bearded lady, the fat man, sword swallowers, snake charmers, and the like. Acts of this kind later became part of the side show, one of the most important parts of the old-time circus.

When Barnum was sixty years old, in 1880, he met James Bailey. Bailey, whose parents were circus performers, had been raised in the circus. At the age of twenty-four, he had become part owner of the Cooper and Bailey Circus, a profitable show that had already toured both Aus-

• •

*A hippodrome is an arena, especially one where horses are raced.

tralia and South America by the time Barnum and Bailey met. In 1881, Barnum merged with Bailey to create the Barnum & Bailey Circus. It was promoted as "The Greatest Show on Earth." The circus became a huge success, largely because of Bailey's thorough knowledge of how to run a circus business.

Barnum and Bailey made many changes in the circus. Bailey understood the importance of good planning and timing in circus shows, and, as a result, Barnum & Bailey performances thrilled audiences in a way no other circus had. Barnum provided the circus with one of its greatest attractions, Jumbo, a gigantic seven-ton elephant that he bought from a London zoo. Barnum and Bailey also added the famous third ring, so productions were bigger and better than ever.

In 1891, Barnum became seriously ill. He asked a New York newspaper to publish his obituary before he died so that he could have the pleasure of reading it. Several weeks later, on April 7, 1891, P.T. Barnum died in his Connecticut home.

Although Barnum did not invent the circus, he gave it a new dimension. He brought a special kind of showmanship and style to the circus, and no one before or since has had as great an effect on the big top as P.T. Barnum.

When Forty Million Americans Saw the Future

BY ENNIS DULING

The wait to get into some exhibits at the 1939–1940 New York World's Fair in Queens was as long as an hour. Children tugged at their parents' hands. Adults shifted from one leg to another and then moved a few feet up a ramp. But to be able to look at the future, it was a relatively short wait.

At the General Motors Futurama, twenty-eight thousand visitors a day rode on moving chairs above a model of America as it might look in 1960. America in the model was greener and cleaner than it was in the 1930s. Cities were places of space, sunshine, and fresh air. Pollution and slums were things of the past. In the country, there were well-kept farms, orchards, forests, and parks. Crisscrossing the land were superhighways where teardrop-shaped cars raced along at one hundred miles per hour.

At the fair's eighteen hundred exhibits, one could see the newest inventions — man-made fabrics, fluorescent lights, plastics, and television — and learn about the advances people were making in medicine, transportation, farming, and more.

The theme of the fair was "Building the World of Tomorrow." The goal was not to guess at the future, but to

> The goal was not to guess at the future, but to help people see real possibilities.

help people see real possibilities. It was an optimistic advertisement for the future. A thousand acres of city dump had been transformed to create the fairgrounds. Ten thousand trees and one million tulips were planted. Fifty-eight foreign countries had come together in peace to hold exhibits.

The best-known buildings were the fair's symbols, the Trylon and the Perisphere. The Trylon was a three-sided needle 610 feet tall (about sixty stories high). Next to it was the Perisphere, a white ball the height of an eighteen-story building.

Inside the Perisphere, visitors looked down on another model of future America called Democracity. A clean city without slums was surrounded by green space and well-planned suburbs and towns. Planning and cooperation were the keys to Democracity. Pollution-free electricity came from a dam holding back the power of a river.

Some critics of the fair argued that the predictions were really gimmicks. But most visitors liked the gimmicks, such as Elektro the Mechanical Man, Voder (a machine that could duplicate human speech), and the birthday celebration for Elsie the Cow at the Dairy of Tomorrow. It would be good if, in the future, polio and smallpox were conquered, there was no more unemployment, and all people were treated fairly and equally. But the fair was mostly a time for fun, not serious thoughts such as these.

Many of the most popular exhibits were in the large amusement area and had nothing to do with the future. At the Parachute Jump, people were hoisted two hundred fifty feet in the air and then dropped. They floated to the ground suspended from a parachute.

Americans must have realized they were looking at the future when they saw some of the first televisions. The screen on the RCA model was tiny (twelve inches from corner to corner), and the price was large (six hundred dollars). But people could stare at the small picture and dream of a future when the invention would be in their homes.

While it looked to the future, the fair overlooked a danger that was already evident. Before the 1939 season ended, World War II had begun in Europe. When the Trylon and Perisphere — symbols of planning and cooperation — were torn down, their steel frameworks were used to build the weapons the United States needed for its war effort.

The Harlem Renaissance

COME WITH US.
IT'S A HOT SUMMER NIGHT IN HARLEM, NEW YORK, 1926.

Finely dressed people from downtown Manhattan are enthusiastically traveling by subway to this neighborhood. Others who live in the area eagerly escape their stuffy apartments. The rhythms and beats of the blues and jazz can be heard from the cabarets and night-clubs. Poetry and drama readings are being held at local libraries. And, at house-rent parties, people donate rent money to laugh and dance the night away to the music of local musicians.

In the 1920s and early 1930s, Harlem was the largest black urban community in the country. Many African Americans had moved there from the South in the two decades since 1900. Harlem was a community of families, homes, and businesses. It also was the spiritual center of the Harlem Renaissance, a 1920s artistic movement made up of black writers,

W.E.B. Du Bois encouraged African Americans to strive for social equality. He was a historian, teacher, sociologist, author, poet, and editor.

poets, dancers, singers, actors, composers, and painters. A renaissance is a rebirth or rediscovery and is often a

Zora Neale Hurston studied and wrote about the folklore of African Americans in the South.

were eager to shed old ideas and accept new ones. Caught up in the excitement of the times, black artists were eager to be heard, and many people listened.

The artists of the Harlem Renaissance were not a formal, organized group. They did not attend scheduled weekly meetings with set agendas or share a common political or philosophical belief. It was this growing black city, Harlem, and their common cultural experience that brought them together. Most of these artists lived in Harlem at one time or another and saw each other on the streets, in the library, and at parties, clubs, formal dinners, and readings. Many were friends.

In the 1930s, when the economy collapsed and times got bad, the Harlem Renaissance lost its momentum. Money was no longer available to support the artists, and Harlem lost its focus as the center of the movement. But the creativity it inspired did not die. The spirit of the renaissance and the enormous body of art it produced have continued to enrich those who enjoy it and to inspire new artists, both black and white.

time when much artistic activity takes place. Black artists in the 1920s were interested not only in rediscovering their African roots and culture but also in understanding their place in American society.

The times — the Roaring Twenties — played a big role in giving these artists the opportunity to voice their black experiences. World War I had just ended; times were better economically for most people, including the black middle class; and people everywhere

Entertainers of the Renaissance

BY SHARI LYN ZUBER

"This joint is jumpin'. It's really somethin'." These words from a Fats Waller song describe the energy that pulsed through Harlem during the 1920s. The prosperity of that era brought about an awakening of black talent in the United States. Chicago, Kansas City, and New Orleans were centers for evolving musical styles such as jazz (music with a strong rhythmic style and complex harmonies that grew from black work songs and spirituals) and the blues (a form of jazz with a slower beat and often melancholy lyrics). But with its growing African American population, Harlem became the mecca for this renaissance.

On the stage, musicals by black composers, starring black singers and dancers, lit up Harlem and Broadway theaters. Bandleaders kept people "stompin' at the Savoy" and other night spots with dances such as the Charleston and the Black Bottom. Teary-eyed audiences listened as blues singers poured out their hearts and stage stars delivered stirring performances. Even the world of opera was opened to blacks because of the talents of Roland Hayes and Marian Anderson.

> On the stage, musicals by black composers, starring black singers and dancers, lit up Harlem and Broadway theaters.

Fats Waller

So settle yourself down in a front-row seat and join us for this review of the performers who brought the Harlem Renaissance to life. Let the show begin!

Composers and Musicians

Noble Sissle and Eubie Blake

Lyricist Noble Sissle and composer James Hubert "Eubie" Blake came from different backgrounds but shared the same dream: to bring their talents to Broadway. Opening in May 1921 on Broadway with a small budget and scenery and costumes left over from failed shows, the all-black musical comedy *Shuffle Along* was a surprise hit. Some claim that the Harlem Renaissance came about because of the musical's success. The show became the prototype (model) for black Broadway musicals. Later Sissle and Blake worked both together and separately. Sissle became a band-leader, and Blake continued performing until the age of one hundred.

W.C. Handy

Traveling with minstrel shows in the late nineteenth century, William Christopher Handy was tired of playing music that caricatured blacks. He decided to play the kind of music he had heard when he was a boy growing up in the South, a combination of spirituals and black work songs. That kind of music came to be called the blues, and Handy was known as the "Father of the Blues." Although audiences enjoyed the music Handy's orchestra played, he was unable to get it published. He eventually formed his own music publishing company and made anthologies of blues songs. Many of Handy's blues compositions, such as "St. Louis Blues" and "Beale Street Blues," have become classics.

Fats Waller

Thomas Wright "Fats" Waller played the piano in true Harlem style. Incorporating ragtime and jazz, he made piano rolls (for player pianos) and adapted his style to the organ. In addition to his jazz pieces, Waller was a popular composer, counting among his many hits "Honeysuckle Rose," "I'm Gonna Sit Right Down and Write Myself a Letter," and "Ain't Misbehavin'." The last of these was first heard in *Hot Chocolates,* a show that went from the Harlem nightspot Connie's Inn to Broadway in 1929. In 1978, a musical revue titled *Ain't Misbehavin'* opened on Broadway and featured many of Waller's songs.

Singers

Florence Mills

Petite Florence Mills won the hearts of her audiences when she began as a child performer. She spent her early years developing her musical comedy talents on the road and in vaudeville with her two sisters. In 1921, she came to Broadway in *Shuffle Along* and became one of the first major black female stars. She went on to star in musicals in New York and Europe, including *Plantation Revue, Dixie to Broadway,* and *Blackbirds.*

Bessie Smith

Bessie Smith, the "Empress of the Blues," had a powerful voice and an original style. Her songs depicted the struggle of black people, often bringing audiences to tears. Her recording career on race records (records by

Bessie Smith

black artists intended for black audiences) began in 1923 with "Down-Hearted Blues" and later included blues classics such as "'Tain't Nobody's Business If I Do" and "Nobody Knows You When You're Down and Out."

Roland Hayes

Prior to the Harlem Renaissance, many people believed that the musical talents of African Americans were limited to nightclubs and comedy revues. Roland Hayes changed that attitude. This superb operatic tenor opened the world of classical music to African Americans and introduced spirituals and black folk music to classical audiences. His concerts in Europe led to his acceptance in the United States, and in 1923 he became the first black to perform at New York's Carnegie Hall. Hayes opened the door for other classical singers, including his protégée, Marian Anderson.

Bandleaders

Fletcher Henderson

Beginning his musical career as a "song plugger" for W.C. Handy's Music Company, James Fletcher Henderson moved on to house pianist for Black Swan records, where Bessie Smith and Ethel Waters also were under contract.

Henderson was an accomplished arranger, and bands such as Benny Goodman's and Tommy Dorsey's were successful in part because of Henderson's work. Henderson's own orchestra played downtown at the white-only Roseland Ballroom, and, for a brief period, he was a member of Goodman's integrated band.

Cab Calloway

Known as the "King of the Hi-De-Ho," Cabell Calloway was one of the few bandleaders who did not play an instrument. His energetic personality and style of singing songs such as "Minnie the Moocher" appealed to audiences. His band played both black-only and integrated clubs and became nationally known on radio and in films. After the big band era, Calloway continued to perform solo, appearing on the Broadway stage, in movies, and on television.

Louis Armstrong

Growing up in New Orleans, Daniel Louis Armstrong heard Dixieland, ragtime, and the blues. He developed his own jazz style on the cornet and trumpet. His gravelly voice inspired others. Armstrong "jazzed" up popular hits such as "Mack the Knife" and "Hello

Duke Ellington

Dolly." He was called "Satchmo,"
"Pops," and "America's Goodwill
Ambassador to the World." His trade-
mark was a white linen handkerchief.

Duke Ellington

Edward Kennedy "Duke" Ellington
headlined at the Cotton Club, and his
orchestra's performances were broad-
cast on radio from coast to coast.
Ellington's orchestra played a "sophis-

ticated" jazz called swing after his song
"It Don't Mean a Thing If It Ain't Got
That Swing."

Dancers

Bill "Bojangles" Robinson

One of the greatest tap dancers of all
time, Bill Robinson was a "born performer" who sang and did comedy
while he danced. His career began in
minstrel shows and progressed to

vaudeville, where he became the first black solo entertainer, although he was never permitted to have top billing. He first appeared on Broadway in *Blackbirds of 1928.* During the Great Depression of the 1930s, Robinson became a movie star, most notably opposite child star Shirley Temple. So beloved was Robinson that he was known as the "Mayor of Harlem."

The Nicholas Brothers

Opening at the Cotton Club when Harold was eight and Fayard was fourteen, the Nicholas Brothers were known as a flash act because of the fancy steps and lightning speed with which they performed. Harold did impersonations, and both brothers sang, tapped, and performed airborne splits. They were able to dance up walls and come off them in splits and backward somersaults. In the 1930s and 1940s, the brothers appeared in white Broadway shows and movies.

Actors

Charles Gilpin

When Charles Gilpin stepped into the role of Brutus Jones in Eugene O'Neill's play *The Emperor Jones,* he astonished the audience with his performance and made theater history.

Until then, dramatic roles for black actors were extremely rare because whites did not believe black performers were able to play serious roles. Hence, Gilpin's early career was limited to county fairs, minstrel shows, vaudeville, and touring acting troupes. He eventually organized the first dramatic theater group in New York, the Lafayette Players, and helped to found an acting company in Cleveland. Thanks to Gilpin, many black actors were given an opportunity to play serious roles.

Paul Robeson

Among the many stars who had their start in the musical comedy *Shuffle Along* was a young law student named Paul Robeson. Robeson later abandoned his law practice for the stage and screen. One of his first plays was Eugene O'Neill's *All God's Chillun Got Wings,* the story of an interracial marriage — a "forbidden" topic in the 1920s. In addition to acting, Robeson had a magnificent singing voice, which he exhibited at club performances, on the stage, and in movies. Robeson spent much of his life trying to achieve equality for African Americans.

Artists in the Making

BY CAROL GELBER

The extra-long school day begins at eight o'clock in the morning for students at Fiorello H. La Guardia High School of the Arts in New York City. Many students have been up since dawn and have traveled by subway for over an hour to get to school. All of them have a double load of schoolwork. Yet each year, thousands of hopeful students apply for one of the places in the freshman class. What makes this school so appealing?

La Guardia High School specializes in training for the visual and performing arts. It is named for the mayor who founded it in 1936 to provide a place where, in his own words, "the most gifted and talented public school students of New York City can pursue their talents in art or music." The 1980 movie *Fame* centered on the experiences of students at the High School for the Performing Arts, now part of La Guardia.

Today the high school has a splendid building at Lincoln Center,

the performing arts center of New York City. Every student is enrolled in one of the school's five departments, called "studios": dance, art, voice, instrumental, and drama. Studio teachers are professional artists, dancers, musicians, and actors. Students spend half of each school day in studio classes and the other half in academic, college preparatory classes (over ninety percent of graduates go on to college).

Every December and January, each of the five studios holds a competitive admissions examination. For example, eighth- or ninth-graders applying to the art studio must take a three-part test in which they draw from a live model, draw a still life from memory, and illustrate a topic such as "a hot day at the beach." In addition, they must show a portfolio of their own artwork — ten to twenty drawings or paintings.

Student artwork hangs in the hallways throughout the school. One student artist said, "Drawing is a skill that I use to express what is on my mind when I can't use words."

Dance students spend many hours in ballet and modern dance classes or exercising in practice studios in front of floor-to-ceiling mirrors. Some of them will become professional dancers; others plan to teach dance.

Artists need good light in which to work. At La Guardia High School, art studios are on the top floors, where walls of windows flood the room with light. Senior students enter their best work in competitive group exhibitions held in the school's large art gallery. Like shows in professional art galleries, these exhibitions open with a party and are always well attended by students, their families, and the school faculty.

Music students practice in the school's soundproof rehearsal rooms. The student symphonic orchestras, jazz bands, and gospel choir often perform in the school's eleven-hundred-seat concert auditorium. In fact, at La Guardia High School, all student assemblies are music, dance, or drama performances.

Student actors learn how to apply stage makeup, as well as how to speak and move on-stage. The student actors put on plays for fellow students in the school's beautiful theater. Admittance to the drama studio is based on audition. Applicants have to perform two short monologues. More than two thousand would-be actors apply to the school every year.

Queens Celebrates the King of Jazz

BY SHARON VATSKY

For more than three decades, Lucille and Louis Armstrong lived on 107th Street in Corona. Everyone in this Queens community knew that Armstrong was world famous, but to the children of Corona, he was simply "Uncle Louis." The neighborhood continues to keep Armstrong's memory alive. Two Queens schools bear his name: P.S. 143, the Louis Armstrong Elementary School (located just blocks from the Armstrong House), and I.S. 227, the Louis Armstrong Intermediate School. In 1977, the Louis Armstrong House became a National Historic Landmark.

From September 22, 1994, to January 8, 1995, Louis Armstrong was on tour again, and his first stop was in his old New York City neighborhood at the Queens Museum of Art. The Smith-sonian Institution Traveling Exhibition Service (SITES) organized the exhibition "Louis Armstrong: A Cultural Legacy," which traced Armstrong's life from a poor boy in New Orleans to an internationally famous jazz musician. Memorabilia, original recordings, and video clips brought Armstrong's personality and music to life.

The exhibition also included paintings, drawings, and photographs by famous artists such as Stuart Davis, Archibald Motley, Jr., Romare Bearden, and Annie Leibovitz. Through the work of these and other visual artists, and with a catalog of essays by noted art and jazz scholars, the exhibition celebrated the legacy of Armstrong and jazz.

Many items for the exhibition were provided by the Louis Armstrong

Louis Armstrong enjoyed playing trumpet with neighborhood boys on the front steps of his home in Corona, Queens.

Archives at Queens College. Other sources of items included the Institute of Jazz Studies at Rutgers University, the Hogan Jazz Archive at Tulane University, the Schomburg Center for Research in New York City, the New Orleans Museum of Art, and the Howard University Gallery of Art in Washington, D.C.

The Louis Armstrong Archives also is located in Queens. When Lucille Armstrong died in 1983, she left boxes of letters, recipes, and photographs to Queens College. After devoting three years to organizing, preserving, and cataloging more than twenty thousand items, the archives opened its doors to the public in May 1994. Visitors and researchers are now offered a personal look at the legendary jazz performer.

The archives has two hundred pages of autobiographical manuscripts in Armstrong's handwriting, thousands of previously unpublished photographs (such as the only known photograph of his father), more than one hundred plaques and awards, trumpets and mouthpieces, scrapbooks filled with Armstrong's fan mail, and dozens of tape recordings of Armstrong telling jokes and stories. The archives displays selected items on a rotating basis, so there is always something new to see.

CITY GAMES

BY LAURA DICKSTEIN,
MUSEUM OF THE CITY OF NEW YORK

How do you play baseball if you do not have a ball field or cannot afford a bat? Children in New York City have traditionally enjoyed the same games as children in suburban and rural areas, but living in the city has forced them to adapt these

Photographer Lewis Hine captured this shot of New York City children using a tenement alley as a ball field.

games to the urban environment. Games such as stickball and stoopball developed this way. They required very little equipment, and their rules and techniques took into account the nature of their particular play area — the city streets.

Stickball, first played in New York City during the 1880s, has rules similar to those for baseball. From the 1880s to the 1920s, New York City's population swelled with new immigrants. During this period, baseball was developing into "America's favorite pastime," and learning the game was considered one of the rituals of becoming an American. Since there were few ball fields in the increasingly crowded urban neighborhoods, immigrant children played the game on the street. The bases included fire hydrants, sewer covers, parked cars, or lampposts. Players used a sawed-off broom or mop handle (a stick) for a bat and a pink rubber ball, called a "spaldeen."

Stoopball is another version of baseball in the city. In the 1850s, many four-story buildings called brownstones were being built with high front steps called a stoop. The game stoopball is played by bouncing a ball off the stoop. The distance the ball bounces determines whether it is a single, double, triple, or home run. Many children preferred this game over stickball because it was safer to play — there was less chance of having to move because of traffic!

Other games played on city streets and sidewalks included marbles, hopscotch, jacks, and skelly. To play skelly, you need crayons, chalk, clay, and one bottle cap per player. The bottle caps are playing pieces. You can press clay into the caps to weight them down so that they will skim nicely along concrete surfaces when flicked with the thumb and forefinger. To create a skelly board, draw a large square in chalk on the sidewalk. Inside the large square, draw smaller squares numbered from 1 to 13. You can arrange the numbers in whatever order you like, but on most boards the odd numbers are diagonally across from the even numbers. Players take turns shooting their bottle caps around the board into each of the boxes in number sequence. The winner is the first player to shoot his or her bottle cap into the thirteenth box.

BOOKS TO READ

Prince of Humbug: The Life of P.T. Barnum *by Cathy Andronik* (Old Tappan, New Jersey: Macmillan Publishing Company, 1994) reveals the big dreams and big schemes of the showman. Grades 4 to 9.

Duke Ellington *by Andrea D. Pinkney* (New York: Hyperion Books for Children, 1998) is a biography of America's great jazz musician and composer, with illustrations by Brian Pinkney. Grade 3 and up.

Broadway Day & Night *by Ken Marsolais* (New York: Pocket Books, 1992) follows actors, directors, and producers from auditions to opening night, with photos and interviews. An adult book that children might enjoy.

MORE MEDIA

P.T. Barnum: American Dreamer. This 47-minute video presents the biography of the famous showman. Contact A&E: (212) 661-4500.

Harlem in the 20s (1971). Harlem's artists, entertainers, writers, and leaders are introduced against the background of the changing Harlem neighborhood. Contact Krasker Memorial Film Library, Boston University: (617) 353-8112.

The Call of the Jitterbug (1989). Old footage and interviews with musicians and dancers recall the colorful era of jazz dancing. Contact Filmakers Library: (212) 808-4980.

PLACES TO VISIT

Museum of Television and Radio. Galleries show photographs, objects, and videos relating to the history of broadcasting. At private viewing stations, you can call up your choice of TV and radio shows from a large collection or sample the museum's "top hits."

Sony Wonder Technology Lab. The first floor of a modern skyscraper features interactive exhibits, including a video game production studio, a sound recording studio, and a television production studio.

American Museum of the Moving Image, Queens. This museum focuses on films and how they are made. You can watch a demonstration on moviemaking topics such as animation and sound editing or view film clips and collections of tools used in film.

Langston Hughes Community Library and Cultural Center, Queens. Posters and African arts are part of the Langston Hughes collection at this library. The Black Heritage Reference Center offers films, festivals, and readings about African Americans.

Index

This Index lists topics that appear in the book, along with the pages on which they are found. Page numbers after a *p* indicate photographs.